"Tim is an accomplished ....p.....cur who
has earned his wisdom by taking risks and building
businesses — his story is inspiring and insightful!"

Wayne E. Bossert
Regional President
RBC Financial Group

"Tim Moore is a Canadian, but his instincts are
those of the classic American entrepreneur. In *You
Don't Need an MBA to Make Millions*, Mr. Moore
exhibits those instincts by recounting dozens of
anecdotes from his career. The anecdotes illustrate
the effectiveness of the business style and practices
which the author has adopted and which he advocates with enthusiasm. Every entrepreneur, whether
aspiring or established, should read this book."

Gil Bennett, Chairman
Canadian Tire Corporation

"People with passion and a vision move mountains.
Tim Moore is one of those entrepreneurs who
succeeds at all he touches thanks to his brilliant
gut-feel style and an understanding that the biggest
asset in life is people. Share your wealth, and the
world is your oyster.

Linda Leatherdale,
Money Editor, *The Toronto Sun* and Host, *Money Line* TV show

"Tim Moore's life story should be read by (or to) young people everywhere who struggle with academic schoolwork but have other strengths — and by their parents as well. Tim proves that entrepreneurial success and social responsibility are not mutually exclusive — in fact, they complement each other. This model success story, written with true honesty, humility, and heart has important lessons for us all."

Dr. Ruth M. Goldbloom, O.C.
Chair, Pier 21 Foundation

"Whether you are just starting out or have been in business for years, you should take note of the characteristics and behaviors Tim Moore uses and describes. This book will have a positive impact on everyone that reads it — Tim's success speaks for itself."

Sarah Dennis
Vice President
The Chronicle Herald, Halifax

"A must-read for any budding entrepreneur. Tim is a great communicator. He really understands the people-business and is one of the best relationship builders I know. His key lessons learned are management jewels."

Dave Martin
District Vice President
Scotia Bank

"I have known Tim Moore for over twenty-five years. Having moved beyond the 'Midnight Rider' years, he is a true entrepreneur with integrity and evident skill, having great respect for his customers and those with whom he works. Those who read this book will learn much, whether they be in business or in any profession where skills are needed to deal with people and attain goals successfully."

Rev. Daniel J. Bohan
Archbishop of Regina

"This book of Tim Moore's is a book of hope. It emphasizes that everyone can achieve their dream. All you have to do is work hard and not lose faith in yourself."

Lillian Morgenthau, President
Canadian Association for the 50 Plus (CARP)

"Tim Moore is a passionate teacher that allows young and aspiring entrepreneurs learn through his mistakes and successes. A great book for all entrepreneurs, aspiring or otherwise."

Mark Borkowski, President
Mercantile Mergers & Acquisitions Corporation

"Chapter headings like 'Forks In The Road,' 'War Stories,' and 'Lessons Learned The Hard Way' sound like tough reading but this fast-paced adventure story of a successful business career is a great inspiration for any entrepreneur. Take the advice; learn from a great achiever how self-confidence, passion, vision, and integrity can make you a winner too."

David Parker
Calgary Business Columnist

"As an athlete I could relate to the message contained in this book. Success in business, as in sport or in any other area, requires an unrelenting commitment to the goals you set for yourself. Written in an easy-to-read style with lots of personal anecdotes, this book is sure to motivate many of its readers to start setting new goals for their future."

Jeremy Wotherspoon
Olympic Medal Speedskater

YOU DON'T NEED AN MBA TO MAKE MILLIONS

SECRETS OF A SERIAL ENTREPRENEUR

TIM MOORE
with Carol Davis and Allan Gould

ECW PRESS

Copyright © Tim Moore, 2005

Published by ECW PRESS
2120 Queen Street East, Suite 200, Toronto, Ontario, Canada M4E 1E2

LIBRARY AND ARCHIVES CANADA CATALOGUING IN PUBLICATION

Moore, Tim, 1944–
You don't need an MBA to make millions: secrets of a serial entrepreneur / Tim
Moore; with Carol Davis & Allan Gould

ISBN 1-55022-694-0

1. New business enterprises — Planning. 2. New business enterprises — Management.
1. Davis, Carol 11. Gould, Allan, 1944– 111. Title.

HD62.5.M667 2005   658.1'141   C2004-907050-9

Cover and Text Design: Tania Craan
Production & Typesetting: Mary Bowness
Printing: Marc Veilleux Imprimeur Inc.

This book is set in Penumbra and Sabon.

The publication of *You Don't Need An MBA To Make Millions* has been generously
supported by the Ontario Media Development Corporation and the Government of
Canada through the Book Publishing Industry Development Program.
Canadä

DISTRIBUTION
CANADA: Jaguar Book Group, 100 Armstrong Avenue, Georgetown, ON, L7G 5S4
UNITED STATES: Independent Publishers Group, 814 North Franklin Street,
Chicago, Illinois 60610

PRINTED AND BOUND IN CANADA

ECW PRESS
ecwpress.com

I owe a debt of gratitude to the thousands of employees and the many partners who have believed in me and who have demonstrated their loyalty, dedication, and affection over the years.

This book is also dedicated to the thousands of corporate clients who took a chance, who gave me an opportunity, and who had confidence in our ability to perform. Many became good friends. Words can never describe my indebtedness to you.

To my four boys, Timmy, Jason, Matthew, and Christopher, my love for you is unwavering. The thought of a life without you in it is unimaginable.

To my beloved wife, Bernardine, for the past 28 years you have been the driving force behind all that I have accomplished. You believed in me, helped me overcome obstacles, and challenged me to become all that I could be. You are my confidante, my greatest supporter, and the love of my life.

To my closest friends, who have made life so meaningful, I thank you.

To my siblings and extended family, I thank you for your love, support, and friendship.

Net proceeds from the sale of this book will be donated to Saint Marys University in Halifax. Two of my sons, Matthew and Christopher, graduated from this fine educational institution and I consider it a privilege to serve as a board member.

ACKNOWLEDGEMENTS

I'd like to thank my dear friend Carol Davis, who spent countless hours helping me write this book. We worked together on my previous book and it was a pleasure to repeat the experience. She listened to my stories and then crafted them into the written word. I know in my heart that if it were not for Carol's courage, tenacity, work ethic, and belief in me, this book most likely would not have come into fruition. Many thanks go to prolific writer Allan Gould, who assisted us on this project. Allan's knowledge and understanding of the publishing world was invaluable to me. He has become a wonderful friend.

I'd also like to thank friends Jeff Morris, Bob Belliveau, and Mark Borkowski, who encouraged, counseled, and guided me throughout the process of putting this book together.

Finally, I'd like to thank Tracey Millen of ECW Press for her excellent recommendations. She provided the expertise that helped my co-authors and I immensely.

INTRODUCTION

"Formal education will make you a living.
Self education will make you a fortune."
— *Jim Rohm*

Do you want to be an entrepreneur, but are afraid to try because you didn't go to business school? As a self-made multi-millionaire, I'm here to tell you that an MBA is *not* a prerequisite to success. I know from personal experience that it is possible to be a successful business owner in spite of this "deficit," and I will share with you what I have learned. Now let's make it clear, I have the highest regard for advanced education, but I also understand that just because people are not academically inclined in their youth, doesn't mean that they are not intelligent or capable of doing well in life — *extremely well.*

Just consider where I came from:

- Failed Grade 3
- Dropped math in Grade 10

- Failed Grade 12, but did manage to repeat it successfully
- Failed Grade 13 with a 35% average
- Was told I didn't have the aptitude or ability for academics

I know I'm not the only one wth such dubious academic credentials. but sometimes, the most unlikely people achieve success. I was speaking to a friend of mine from high school recently about this very subject. He commented on the fact that the three people from our senior year class who were considered to be least likely to succeed because of poor academic performance have all done very well in life. I took the entrepreneurial road and the other two joined major corporations and moved up the ranks to become President and CEO of their respective organizations. (All three of us have become multi-millionaires.)

Early on, I was labelled "most unlikely to succeed." How then did I go from academic failure to successful entrepreneur, with a net worth of millions of dollars? Did I inherit money? No. Did I go into the family business? No. Instead, I did it the old-fashioned way by:

- Working hard
- Taking risks
- Making sacrifices
- Developing street smarts
- Learning from other successful people
- Putting my heart and soul into my business
- Being generous
- Delivering exceptional value to customers
- Never giving up

From my earliest days as the sole owner of a small Montreal-based moving company, to the 22 years spent building the largest, coast to coast moving company in the country (AMJ Campbell Van Lines), and then on to the creation of Premiere Executive Suites, a highly successful, national extended-stay accommodation business, I have put these tenets into practice on a daily basis. Each of these three businesses started out small and yet they grew to become extremely profitable and well respected. I cherish the years spent growing and nurturing these companies. As the years passed, I matured as an entrepreneur and it is the wisdom gained from these experiences that I want to pass on to other aspiring entrepreneurs, who just need a little encouragement to make that leap from dreaming to doing. I will introduce you to a number of talented individuals who had the courage to become entrepreneurs. These men and women came from many walks of life, but what they had in common was a burning desire to be in charge of their own destiny. They hungered for success and were prepared to work hard to achieve it. If asked, they will tell you their only regret is that they didn't become entrepreneurs sooner.

A few of these individuals didn't start believing in themselves until I showed them I had faith in their abilities. Eventually, they gained the necessary confidence to take the next step. As an example, when we decided to franchise most of our moving company offices, we approached the existing managers to give them the first right of refusal for their location. One of our managers, David Way, had been doing an extraordinary job with his branch in Edmonton, Alberta. It was very well run, and he had assembled an outstanding team of employees.

However, when offered the opportunity to become a franchisee, he was somewhat reluctant. I remember him saying to me, with some irritation, "So, what you are telling me is that I have to buy my job!" I told him that no one was forcing him to do so. If he didn't want to become an owner, then we would find another spot for him in the company as an employee. In the end, he decided to become a franchisee, and he will tell anyone who asks him today that it was the best decision he ever made. He had total control over his operation, and even better, he made more money. Much, much more.

Entrepreneurship can be very rewarding, in terms of money, personal satisfaction, and a sense of control over your life. Some people will say that it is crass to put money first on the list of rewards, but I don't agree with them. Frankly, I am proud that I have managed to make millions of dollars from my various business ventures. Why else would someone go into business, if not to make money? In spite of what some people might tell you, a desire to earn more money is a valid reason. It's one of the things that motivated me in the beginning, and to be honest, still motivates me. Money is tangible proof of your ability to succeed in business. Obviously, money also gives you a sense of security; it provides for your family, and allows you to enjoy some of the finer things in life. Helping others less fortunate is also a very satisfying way to spend some of your hard-earned money.

Being an entrepreneur is not easy, but from my experience and that of many others, I can tell you unequivocally that it is a very exciting career choice. So *don't listen to people who try to talk you out of becoming an entrepreneur, and who tell you that you will fail.* It isn't their place to make this judgement. It's your life, and while you may value the opinion of others, it is important for you to make your own decision based on what *you* really want out of life. You are in control of your own destiny.

A business associate from Halifax, Fred Connors, runs a successful salon and spa business called Fritsa Design Incorporated. Over the years, I have seen Fred build his business to new levels through his personal drive and creativity. When asked how you create a successful enterprise, Fred explained:

> In the most basic sense, the creation of a business is easy. However, the creation of a great business can be just as easy if one possesses drive. This drive cannot just be for success. The drive of a successful businessperson encompasses striving for excellence and an inherent inner-drive to constantly maintain and achieve both personal and business goals. This drive also includes the delicate balance of a constantly evolving vision, coupled with a commitment to remain true to the instincts that prompted the vision in the first place.
> Good ideas and great businesses fall by the wayside because passion and vision become obscured by the enormity of hard work. Being a successful businessperson is a dichotomy in the truest sense — one side is welcoming and accommodating while the other is realistic and able to decisively make the hard choices regarding the best interests of the business. There is a fine balance between talent, passion, and an ability to handle the tremendous workload of a business.
> Maintaining this balance is the key that allows one to achieve goals, realize success, and be creatively fulfilled.

If I had listened to the naysayers in my life (especially the ones from my early days in school), I might never have tried to do better. Instead, I chose to be successful, and was prepared to do whatever it took to make that happen. I was determined to overcome any obstacle. When I started out as an entrepreneur, I was 28 years old and $20,000 in debt. However, I knew that I wanted to be a success, and so I set a very ambitious goal for myself: I wanted to become a millionaire by age 40. Well, I made it, and I didn't stop there. In fact, I've spent the last three decades achieving one goal after another. I call it my "A Dream is a Goal with a Deadline" philosophy of business.

I am a firm believer in setting time-specific goals. Many people talk about their dreams for a better future, but unless they create an action plan that includes a deadline, their dreams may never be realized. "Someday" is not specific enough. You must decide what you want, when you expect to get it, and then develop a plan to make it happen. Achieving a goal doesn't happen by chance. You need a plan, even if it is one that involves several stages to reach your goal. It can be as simple as saying, "I want to grow my sales by 10% each year for the next 5 years" or "I want to increase my net worth to X dollars by December 2006." Approaching your dreams in this manner can be a powerful incentive.

Becoming an entrepreneur is a laudable goal in and of itself. And frankly, the world needs more entrepreneurs. In a 1999 speech, British Prime Minister Tony Blair said, "Entrepreneurship will become a core skill which all of our young people will need to exploit the opportunities emerging from science, technology, culture, and communications. Small businesses are an important part of our economy." I have to tell you, I get an incredible amount of satisfaction from seeing a small business grow to become a leader in its industry. I also have a real sense of pride in those individuals whom I have mentored and who have become successful entrepreneurs in their own right.

A friend of mine, Jim Lockington, president of Royal LePage Relocation Solutions, once told me I am a "serial entrepreneur." At a time when other businesspeople are looking forward to retirement, I find myself in the process of launching yet another business. My partners and I fully expect that our new company, Premiere Van Lines, will be a household name within three to five years. Right out of the gate, we had over 30 offices opening simultaneously in April 2005 and upwards of $50 million in revenue. Once again, I am using a business model that is based on sound principles that have worked for me and can work for you too. To use an old cliché, "If *I* can do it, *anyone* can."

I hope that the stories, advice, and suggestions contained in this book will help you become the successful entrepreneur that you were meant to be.

CHAPTER ONE

FORKS IN THE ROAD

"There are moments in life when the door
opens and lets the future in."
— *Deepak Chopra*

My road to entrepreneurship had a few twists and turns. I believe that every life experience teaches you a lesson — even unpleasant experiences or tough times have value. Your character is shaped by your accomplishments, your failures, and what you've learned along the way. I have been successful in business in spite of the fact that I had a less than auspicious beginning. One lesson I've learned is that one can succeed regardless of what appear to be insurmountable obstacles.

In my youth, I was told repeatedly that I lacked any academic aptitude or ability. My home life was stressful, due in part to my father's ongoing financial problems, and the strain they put on the entire family. Consequently, my parents were preoccupied with their own challenges, so they couldn't help me with mine. The combination of problems at home and at school, coupled with the usual teenage angst over my appearance and lack of social skills, was simply overwhelming. I'm sure it won't come as a surprise when I tell you that I had very little self-esteem. Fortunately for me, I discovered the joy of sports. It was the one place where I could excel, and so I gave it my all. Sporting achievements gave me that much-needed boost of esteem. Sports also taught me some valuable lessons about leadership, team building, and determination, which I later applied in business and in life in general. If you have ever played sports, I think you can relate to the value gained from this experience.

My friend Dr. Richard Zuliani, an industrial psychologist now devoted to the field of Executive Coaching, had this to say about how I was able to do well in business in spite of my academic failures:

> It's true that Tim didn't do well in school, but he was well liked and really excelled at team sports. I can't say that I ever envisioned he would end up with the kind of business success he has achieved, but I always figured he'd find his niche. I believe that many of his personal attributes came to the forefront once he decided what he wanted to do with his life. While he didn't focus on his studies, on the sports field he was a very determined and competitive person, attributes he would later need as an entrepreneur.
>
> He may not have gone to business school but he has good business sense. Tim is a very inquisitive person and gathers information from whomever he meets, and he's not afraid to ask for advice. I've also been impressed by Tim's ability to motivate people. By boosting their self-esteem and helping them succeed in their own right he earns their respect and loyalty, which can be a rare commodity in many companies. Although he is sometimes too trusting and consequently a

few people have taken advantage of him, when this happens he deals with it head on and then just puts it in the past. The fact that he can do this frees up his energy to pursue new endeavours. I've no doubt that his new moving business will turn out to be a huge success.

In addition to the positive outcome of participating in sports, some of my salvation came from the priests who taught me in high school and who recognized that I was in need of guidance. I will always be grateful for their subtle encouragement and suggestion that I spend some time at St. Augustine's Seminary, rather than just quit school. It was during the months spent in that cloistered, contemplative environment that I was able to take control of some of my inner demons. This time away from the pressure I had been under both at home and in school was a welcome respite. I felt contented and safe for the first time in my young life. The priests at the seminary were patient with me, and encouraged me in my studies.

Under their tutelage, I started to excel at academic pursuits. At one point, I seriously considered staying on to become a priest. Then many of my friends left and I began to feel rather lonely and cut off from the world. I learned a lot about humility and compassion (which I would later put into practice in both my professional and personal life), but slowly realized that I didn't have a real calling for the priesthood. The time spent there had helped heal my troubled spirit, and I felt that I could focus on making something of myself.

Thirty-five years later, I was at a reception in honour of my brother-in-law's elevation from a priest to a Bishop of the Church. Standing beside the bar, I saw a man coming towards me. He looked vaguely familiar, but I couldn't recall his name. I knew he must be a Bishop from his attire. As he got closer, he said to me, "Is your name Tim?" It was at that moment that I remembered his name was Richard Greco, and he had been one of my classmates at St. Augustine's Seminary. We talked about the past and "different roads taken." I jokingly said to him, "You mean I, too, could have become a Bishop if I had stayed at the seminary?" I was pleased to have this opportunity to talk to someone from that period. It brought back many good memories about an experience that was truly a turning point in my life.

I also came away from my time in the seminary with an abiding respect for anyone in the teaching profession. While I was there, I decided I wanted to become a teacher so I could help others the way I had been helped. It was during this same period that my self-esteem got another well-needed boost. In those days, a university degree was not required to teach elementary school, so I applied for a teaching position. At the interview, the principal told me that I had exceptional communication skills. I was thrilled. This was the first real compliment that I had ever received for something other that my athletic prowess. It was an immediate boost to my confidence. This incident taught me an important message about the power of giving sincere compliments. Since then I have made it a point to compliment others. This practice helps to motivate employees and cement personal relationships. One should never underrate the value of saying something nice to others.

The interview went extraordinarily well, and much to my surprise I was immediately hired. I then spent 18 truly happy months teaching seventh graders at a school in Sudbury, Ontario. I loved teaching, and from the comments I received from my students, their parents, and my principal, I was good at it. Somehow, I instinctively understood how to achieve the right balance between love and discipline, which I practiced later in business and as a parent. This affirmation of my abilities gave me the confidence I had been lacking up until this point in my young life. I encouraged my students and, in turn, they excelled at their studies. Later, I used this same approach with employees and usually got positive results. It's actually quite amazing how far a little encouragement and appreciation can go towards improving performance. The phrases "You did a great job" and "Thank you" are magical management tools. Unfortunately, they are used far too infrequently by even savvy managers. I loved motivating my students to do better. I got a great deal of satisfaction from their successes. Later on as an entrepreneur, I gained this same satisfaction from helping my employees achieve their full potential.

The only downside was that teaching elementary school for $6,000 per year didn't exactly excite me. Having come from a family that struggled under a burden of debt, financial security was important to me. I knew that if I went back to school and earned more credits, my pay would increase, and so that is what I did, first at Waterloo Lutheran (now Wilfred Laurier) in Waterloo, where a combination of part-time and full-time studies eventually led to an honours degree in History. Interestingly enough, the only course I didn't do well in was marketing, where my grade was a D, in sharp contrast to my other courses where I earned A's.

I guess school marks don't always tell the whole story, do they? Then I moved to Montreal in 1971 and enrolled at McGill University for graduate studies. It was my intention to upgrade my qualifications further and then return to the classroom at a higher pay grade. However, once again I reached that proverbial fork in the road and the direction I took this time led me into the world of entrepreneurship.

Unlike most people, I didn't plan to become an entrepreneur. I simply needed to make money to pay for school and somehow I ended up running my own business instead of working for someone else. A fellow from school told me that he had earned a lot of money during the summer school break doing small moves with his pickup truck. People in that city were very mobile, which meant there was no shortage of work for movers. In fact, in those days, all apartment leases expired on May 1, creating a moving bonanza for people in the business. This information piqued my interest. He made it sound so easy I decided that, even if it meant taking some time off from school, it would be worth it in the end. How's *that* for career planning? Now, in this situation, most people would go look for a job with an established moving company. However, I chose not to apply for any jobs, deciding instead to go it alone. Somewhere deep inside me was that entrepreneurial spark just waiting for a chance to spring to life. So, being the optimistic, determined individual that I was and still am, I immediately sold my little Volkswagen, borrowed $2,000 from a bank, and purchased a small pickup truck. Suddenly, I was an entrepreneur — although I had not the slightest clue about running a business! This was going to be the ultimate "learn by doing" experience, and for some strange reason I was more excited than scared.

In my case, there were some very important lessons from my early years that influenced how I would approach the world of business and life in general. Specifically, I learned that it is imperative to really *focus on what you want to achieve.* It's not enough just to be intelligent. There are many smart people who never achieve their dreams, because they don't focus strongly enough. You have to know what you want, how much you are prepared to sacrifice to get it, and how you will go about making it happen. Some people make the mistake of thinking that success will find them, just because they are so naturally intelligent and thus deserving of greatness. They wait, and wait, and wonder why nothing changes in their life. They don't understand that *you have to go after what you want.* In my case, when I decided to go into the moving business, I was determined to do whatever it took to make a success of this venture. To me, that meant earning a lot of money for my efforts. Despite what some people might say, money is a good motivator!

Although I knew next to nothing about the moving business, I knew enough to realize I had to look the part. This is where the concept of *appearing to be confident* comes in to play. People gravitate towards confident individuals and this includes customers. If you are going to own a business, you must learn to display an aura of confidence, even if you are unsure of your own abilities. In time, you will gain real confidence as you mature as an entrepreneur. But right from the start, you must look and act the part, otherwise customers and competitors won't take you seriously.

In my case, it was a little hard to mirror my competitors since I had such limited resources, and for the most part they were well-established moving companies with proper warehouses and fleets of trucks. Obviously I couldn't compete in the normal sense, but I did what I could to get started and expanded my operation gradually as the profits rolled in. My first step was to turn my little pickup truck into a small moving van, by installing a kind of box on the bed of the truck, with steel bars, wood slats, and a tarp. This would protect the furniture from the elements — and Montreal is renowned for its weather, especially in winter. With this setup I could move two rooms of furniture on a single trip. I can't tell you how proud I was of my first moving truck, although I'm sure it elicited many snickers from my competitors.

The next order of the day was to find customers. Because I was such an amateur operation, I understood that I needed a marketing hook, so I decided I would play up the "university student" angle. Most people were impressed when a young person was prepared to work hard, so I recruited big, strong, clean-cut, attractive university students to work with me, and I put them in identical uniforms. We looked like professional movers and to some degree that gave us the confidence we needed to act the part. I placed small ads in local community newspapers, such as *The McGill Daily* and the *N.D.G. Monitor*. In my ads I made it clear that my rates were cheaper than those of my competitors. I figured this would appeal to potential customers.

When you start out in business, it is important to **charge less for your service or product than what is being charged by the competition.** Don't be greedy.

You can always raise your rates once you are established. I used this approach successfully in the moving business and I did it again when I started Premiere Executive Suites in 1999. To give you an example, we charged $1,300 a month for a 550-square-foot furnished condo in Halifax, with all the amenities. This worked out to $40 per night, which was considerably less than what was being charged by other companies in the industry. However, pricing it this way gave us a higher occupancy ratio, which covered our costs and still provided us with a profit. At the same time, we went out of our way to provide extra value to our clients thus earning us an excellent reputation. This approach helped us get established in the field and before long we were able to increase our rates.

My advertisements weren't exactly award-winning copy. As I recall, they read something like this:

Make One "Moore" Move

Then Compare – We Care!

Reliable Student Movers

Cheap Rates – Call 000-0000

Strangely enough, this type of advertisement worked. My telephone rang constantly. Before I knew it I was making more money for two days of moving than I had been receiving for a full week of teaching. Then I got the idea of doing double shifts for that peak moving week in May, when there weren't enough trucks in the city to service all the moves. To the best of my knowledge, I was the only mover in Montreal to take this approach. Customers loved the idea of being able to move when it was convenient. Money was literally pouring in. It was addictive.

Now, the idea of returning to school, and then the classroom, wasn't quite so appealing. I was in my element, running my own business, making my own rules, and answering to no one but myself, and since I was young and healthy, I didn't mind the hard physical labour and the brutal hours. However, my will was tested when I received two teaching offers within a few months of starting my moving business. The lure of security was enticing, but by then, I knew I had a flare for entrepreneurship, and so I turned them down. I was committed to my new way of life.

Right from the start, I wanted to prove to people that I would go out of my way to provide excellent customer service. You might even call it "extreme customer service." I was prepared to do just about anything to make my customers happy. I must have been doing something right, because 70% of my business came from referrals. Even after 5 years in the business, I was probably the only mover in Montreal who didn't have an advertisement in the Yellow Pages. I was so naïve, I didn't even realize that I should be advertising there. Anyone who is in business knows that referrals are the best way to grow your enterprise. Happy customers tell 20 others and before you know it, you have new customers. However, I think every businessperson can tell you at least one horror story about being taken advantage of by a customer. One stands out in my mind that I'd like to share, as it is quite funny.

It involved a woman who called to ask what it would cost to move seven or eight cartons from one residence to another, a few blocks away. I told her that I would do it for $7. I figured it would take me a half-hour at most. (Remember, this was more than 30 years ago.) My first problem came when I discovered I had to go into the underground parking garage of her apartment building. I didn't think about the height of the box on the back of my truck. The result was about a hundred dollars in damage to my homemade moving van. But that one was *my* fault.

I arrived at the apartment and discovered that she had two-and-a-half rooms of furniture to be moved, not the few cartons she had described on the telephone. When I mentioned this to her, she abruptly said, "No, everything goes." I loaded everything on my truck and on the ride over to her new apartment, I tried to raise the issue of payment. I told her that $7 wasn't enough, but I had barely gotten the words out of my mouth when she went totally berserk, shouting and screaming at me. I was almost expecting her to physically attack me, that's how out of control she was. I decided to take my losses and just get the job done.

I should have learned my lesson, but it didn't end there. Three months later, she called me and said she needed her furniture moved again. A sensible person would have said that his company was too busy, but I wasn't one to turn down a paying customer, even a crazy one. However, I was now three months smarter, so I told her that I would have to charge her by the hour, plus my travelling time. She agreed, and paid me at the end of the job, late on a Friday evening. I was relieved at how well things had gone, in contrast to my first experience with this customer. I should have known it was too good to be true.

Late the next evening, I was at home, taking some well-deserved rest, when the telephone rang. It was my favourite customer, who started to shriek about a broom that I had missed taking out from behind a door. I tried to reason with her, by telling her she had some responsibility to leave her items where they would be visible. But, like my first experience with her, she wouldn't listen to reason. This time, she threatened to report me to the Better Business Bureau and the *Montreal Star*. Then she hung up on me. I didn't want any trouble. I had a good thing going with my business, but I didn't have insurance or an operating permit, so the last thing I needed was someone investigating me. I quickly went out and retrieved her beloved broom.

This story became a bit of a legend around AMJ Campbell, and was often repeated, like folklore. One year, we had a Corporate Client Appreciation night. One of our guest speakers for the function was a well-known hockey player, Eddie Shack. He was known to use rather colourful language, so I made a point of talking to him in advance, warning him not use any inappropriate language. "We have a lot of important guests coming," I told him, concerned that they would be offended if he behaved badly. Before Eddie spoke, I told the "broom story," which everyone found amusing.

However, when the NHL player got up to the microphone, he just couldn't resist, and told the audience, in very explicit terms, exactly where he would have told this customer to put her broom. The room exploded in laughter.

The lesson I learned from that experience was a valuable one. From that day forward, I never let a customer intimidate me — if I was in the right. Of course, all business owners know that it is sometimes necessary to make compromises or concessions for the sake of customer goodwill. However, some customers will try to push the envelope on occasion, and you will need all your skills in diplomacy to counter their challenge without losing them as a customer. It's been my experience that unreasonable customers will back down when you firmly but politely refuse to give in to their demands. If done with sufficient tact, you can usually offer up some small concession that will allow them to save face. Most people recognize when they have gone too far with their complaints or demands and are grateful to be given a way to resolve the situation without it becoming too acrimonious. You just have to be prepared to put your own spin on that old adage "a customer is always right," otherwise you could find yourself becoming unprofitable. Of course, you want happy customers, *but not necessarily at any price.*

When you first go into business, you are going to make some mistakes. That's to be expected. The trick is to *learn from your mistakes.* Occasionally, a customer will attempt to take advantage of you. Other times, your own lack of experience will be to blame. You have to chalk these situations up to experience and not dwell on them or allow them to erode your confidence. I've certainly made my share of blunders, especially in my early days in business. One of the worst occurred when I had only been in business for a week. A prospective customer called me and asked how much it would cost to move two-and-a-half rooms of furniture from Boston to Montreal. Because I was a total neophyte to the moving business, I had absolutely no idea what to charge. I told him I would get back to him. I called around to a few of the major van line movers and found out that it would be at least $400. So, being the eager, new entrepreneur, I called the customer back and told him I would do it for $45, plus the cost of gas. And to make the offer even more enticing, I agreed to take him along with me in the truck so he wouldn't have any personal travel expenses. Needless to say, he accepted my quote.

Little did I know this would become a move to remember in more ways than one. There I was, driving down to Boston with the customer beside me in the truck, through the worst blizzard imaginable. Halfway there, he turned to me and said, "Gee Tim, I'm really glad you are doing this for me. It was going to cost me about $300 to do it myself with a rental truck." The 750-mile return trip took 24 hours because of the storm. Not only did I lose money, I could have lost my life on those treacherous roads. Talk about a learning experience. In spite of situations like these, I quickly learned that I liked being in business for myself. Within the first year, not only did I pay off my first loan, I purchased three more pickup trucks, and renamed my company TC Moore Transport. Capitalism in action!

It was also during this period that I discovered the world of real estate and the importance of diversifying your investments. Even as a relatively small entrepreneur, I made a point of using some of my excess cash to buy investment properties, thus ensuring that all of my financial eggs were not in one basket. Much of my wealth has come from this approach. I will elaborate on this idea in a later chapter so that you can learn more about this valuable wealth management tool.

Over the next few years, I grew the company's sales, purchased six additional trucks, and found myself operating a thriving business. I also found that the kind of praise and encouragement I had applied to my students in the classroom worked equally well with my employees. I was very proud of these young men who worked hard and did their best for our customers. My company's success was directly related to how well my employees performed. As I always say, "Good employees will make you money. It is important to treat them well."

To be a success in business, you must learn how to motivate and inspire others. Doing so will increase their confidence level, which will translate itself into a better performance. I would even argue that the ability to motivate and inspire others is critical. It simply isn't possible to build a successful business without help. You will accomplish so much more when all members of your team are committed to achieving the same goals. Dedicate time and energy to nurturing your employees and you will quickly find that human beings are generally capable of a higher level of achievement than they realize. They will rise to the challenge if they believe you are genuinely interested in helping them develop their own unique talents.

I gained a lot of valuable experience during the six years I spent running TC Moore; however, a time came when I started to question if this was what I wanted to do for the rest of my life. I think I was a little frustrated with the fact that I had taken the company as far as it could go. It was still only a local moving company and I just wasn't sure what else I could do to take it to the next level. I was also a bit burnt out from my crushing load of responsibility, and the endless hours of extremely hard work. I had also become engaged and feared that my fiancée Bernardine might change her mind about marrying a man who worked around the clock. What kind of life would that be for her? So, the timing was right to sell the business. In 1977, I sold the company to two of my employees, and left with $80,000. I planned, once again, to return to teaching.

There are several lessons that can be learned from my experiences as a fledgling entrepreneur. One is that, as a company grows to a certain size, it is not always possible to run it totally on your own. You either need a partner, or a few outstanding employees who have complementary skills to your own. The second one is about honing your instincts as they relate to timing. A good businessperson knows when the time is right to make changes. Occasionally, a business reaches its optimal size, and you have to decide if the investment required to take it to the next level is justified, or if you are better off taking your profits and moving on to something new.

What happened to my company after I sold it is another important lesson for new entrepreneurs. The two employees who purchased the company made the mistake of thinking that being business owners meant they could use the company's bank account as their personal money tree. They decided they no longer had to work very hard. This resulted in not only their own poor performance but in reduced productivity from employees who were used to a boss who was a good role model. The combination of poor work habits, lack of re-investment in the operation, and taking too much money out of the company came home to roost when they had to declare bankruptcy within two years of buying the business.

KEY LESSONS LEARNED

- Early failures can be overcome
- Accept help from others when it is offered
- Once you discover what you are good at, work hard to develop those talents
- Sometimes you have to go with your "gut" instincts when making decisions
- Learn to motivate yourself and others
- When starting out, price your product or service below that of your competition
- Find a marketing hook to distinguish you from the competition
- Provide top-notch customer service
- Invest some of your money in a secondary area
- Know when it is time to change direction
- Don't bleed the company coffers dry

MIDNIGHT
DRIVER

"Unless you enter the tiger's den, you cannot take the cubs."
— *Japanese Proverb*

Every entrepreneur is required to take risks. This is part of creating and running a business. Most will be calculated risks, where you have a good idea of the consequences, should things not work out. Others fall more into the "taking a chance" category. I doubt many of my readers will be faced with the types of dilemmas I encountered in my early days as an entrepreneur. As you know, I began the moving business simply because a friend told me it was an easy way to make money. I had no license, no insurance, no capital, and no guarantee of landing any moving jobs. In truth, there was absolutely no structure to my business; I had no concept of five-year plans, or even a one-month plan, as I had no MBA or anything close to it. As a result, I conducted my first business in a rather unorthodox manner.

I certainly wouldn't advocate that you follow my example and play fast and loose with government regulations or start a business without a plan, but I do think it is important for new entrepreneurs to be prepared to face situations that require thinking outside the box. Each business owner will encounter their own challenges depending on the type of business they run. If you are part of an established franchise organization, you will have the advantage of a structured operation with its own systems, rules, and regulations that must be followed. This will make it easier for the fledgling entrepreneur. If, on the other hand, you have started your business from scratch, you will have to make your own decisions when faced with a variety of situations. Occasionally, this will mean that you, too, may circumvent a few rules in order to survive.

While you might question why I would be willing to divulge some of the things I've done in the name of business, I think this information will illustrate my unrelenting desire to survive and succeed as an entrepreneur. Most of the more controversial practices took place in my earliest days, when I could honestly plead ignorance of the rules. However, to this day, I will fight like a tiger when I believe I'm in the right, or if I want something enough to battle for it. I want you to understand that I am *not* advocating illegal activities, and I do recognize that times have changed. However, I want you as entrepreneurs, or aspiring ones, to understand that if you are genuinely committed to becoming successful, you have to push the envelope on occasion, otherwise your business may suffer. Or, to put it another way, "You can't make an omelette without breaking a few eggs."

For me, it was sheer survival. I needed money, and was prepared to do whatever I had to do to get it —

without using a gun and a mask! I was a renegade, that's for sure, but I was also a hard-working one. Knowing little about operating a business didn't deter me even though the cost of *legitimate* entry into the moving business was totally out of my reach. In those days, moving was a highly regulated industry. Local movers had to pay approximately $5,000 for a license. Long-distance moving required an inter-provincial operating authority that could cost up to $200,000. Movers were also required to have adequate fleet and contents insurance. Obviously, I didn't have the money to comply with these regulations — but that didn't stop me from going into business as a mover.

I recall one of my first moves, when an elderly woman called me to move a very expensive antique bedroom suite. It had been her grandmother's, and she was paranoid about it getting damaged, particularly the antique mirror. I told her that I was a professional, and knew exactly how to handle the pieces. When she asked if I was insured, I replied in the affirmative. What I neglected to tell her was that I was *self*-insured (meaning, if I damaged anything, I'd pay for it). Today, I believe this type of information should be disclosed to customers by law. Unlike regular movers, there was no insurance company or van line in the background to complain to if a customer wasn't happy with my settlement. But I was young and optimistic, and I was sure that a claim wouldn't become a reality.

When I arrived at the residence, the woman again stressed the value and importance of the mirror. I assured her everything would be fine. I proceeded to load the truck, putting the furniture in first, followed by two mattresses. Finally, it was time to load the mirror. Being as careful as I possibly could, I placed it on the truck and leaned it against the mattresses, where I was sure it would be safe. Unfortunately, I didn't know that I should have placed the mirror between the two mattresses. As I jumped out of the truck, the mirror shifted slightly away from the mattresses, and hit a solid piece of furniture, breaking. I was just devastated. Understandably, the customer was furious, but to my credit, I paid to have it properly repaired, although I didn't have the money to spare. From that point on, it was a blur of almost around-the-clock days of doing my best to make a living, and keep out of trouble.

My real rule breaking began when I started to get calls from people for moves out of the province, mostly to Ontario. I accepted these jobs, in spite of the fact that I lacked a license for this type of moving. The big problem I had here was getting past the Ministry of Transport weigh scales that are located at certain intervals on the highway. Any truck carrying commercial cargo is required to stop to be weighed, and to have their documentation inspected. Being caught without a proper license was a very serious infraction, with hefty fines and even the possibility of having your truck impounded. A sensible person would have decided that the risk was just too great, but not me. I decided to become a "Midnight Driver," passing by the scales after they closed each evening at 11 p.m. At one point, I even considered painting my truck black, in honour of my renegade status — or of my future, had I been caught.

Not only was I prepared to take risks, I'm afraid I involved some of my family members. I recall the time when my brother Terry and his future wife, Lynne, came to Montreal to help me do some moving for a few days. I asked Terry to load up my pickup truck and take a load to Toronto. Now remember, I did not have an operating license for out of province moving, but I did have a customer who needed a move done so I figured it was worth the risk. Unlike my midnight moves with larger trucks I was sure Terry would be safe. Who would bother to pull over a small pickup truck? Even if they saw furniture on board, they would assume that it was a personal move, not a commercial endeavour.

So Terry got it all loaded and the last piece on was a single mattress that he pushed along the top of the truck. Terry, Lynne, and our customer headed off to Toronto. Just outside of Kingston, Terry looked at the side mirror and noticed a police car with a mattress on top and a side bed-rail protruding. You can imagine his trepidation when the police pulled him over. Visions of fines or worse must have passed through his mind. Imagine his surprise when the two officers asked if he had lost these items. When he responded in the affirmative, they offered to help get them back on the truck. In his most sincere voice, Terry thanked them profusely and went on his way, relieved that they hadn't bothered to ask him any questions. Another close call, not soon forgotten.

When I started out with my small moving company in Montreal, I couldn't afford to pay for commercial office space so I initially operated TC Moore Moving from my basement apartment in NDG. I was paying $15 per week in the early 1970s, which was a bargain even in those days. Later, I moved to a larger one-bedroom apartment on Madison Avenue in the same area, but I continued to use my residence as my place of business for quite some time, in spite of the fact there were by-laws prohibiting this practice.

Of course, being in the moving business meant I had to have some place to park my trucks, which is why most movers had a warehouse/office complex with a compound for vehicles. Since I didn't have that luxury I would tell my men to park the trucks on De Maisonneuve Boulevard and walk over to my apartment to receive their instructions and the paperwork for the moves they were scheduled to handle. It wasn't long before I had four or five trucks in my fleet and upwards of 20 men coming to my apartment on a daily basis. Fortunately I had a great relationship with the superintendent. But even he became a little uneasy about the degree of activity, especially since the other tenants began to complain with increasing frequency.

Eventually I had to move into a small warehouse. Before you get the idea that I had moved up in the world with fancy new digs, let me explain that my first 2,000-square-foot warehouse was the most rundown, dilapidated old place imaginable. We literally used to catch large rats, but I needed a facility and the rent was reasonable. When I think back on those days, I find it hard to believe what I was prepared to endure to make my business a success. However, the end justified the means.

Sometimes, history has a way of repeating itself. Back in 2001, my son Matthew, who was 22 years old, started Moore Moving in Halifax. A good friend of ours, Larry Pringle, who is an international lawyer, had asked Matthew to move some furniture from New York to Toronto. This was less than a month after 9/11, and New York was a minefield for even the most experienced movers. There were whole sections of lower Manhattan where trucks weren't allowed. Access was

very limited and controlled. I also knew that Matthew didn't have a license for cross-border moving, so I was really against the idea. I told him not to do it, but he went anyway. Shades of my early days, heading to a strange city with no concept of where anything was, let alone what the conditions were, with all that post-9/11 activity going on.

He arrived in New York, with his helpers, all of them dressed in full uniform including ties, and carried out a totally professional move — even with all the security, police, and fire trucks on every corner. Larry was extremely appreciative of the fine service. Matthew drove for almost 24 hours before he arrived back in Toronto to deliver the furniture. I would say "like father, like son," but with one difference: I learned something from *him*. He had purchased a trip permit, so that he was legal. I wasn't aware that such a thing existed, so maybe it's true that each successive generation gets a little smarter.

Another piece of irony was that my son's very first move was a load of furniture to Boston. When he told me about it, I was against him doing it since I still had a vivid recollection of my own trip of horrors so many years ago. But times have certainly changed as he pointed out to me after completing the job successfully. "The difference between us," Matthew said, "is that you got $45 and lost money but I made $1,500 and had a profit."

I had a number of close encounters in those early days. After about three years in business, I was starting to get a reputation as a good independent mover, and this certainly kept my phone ringing. One day, I got a request to load a shipment out of a competitor's warehouse. I no sooner pulled away from their yard, than I was pulled over by a Department of Transport vehicle. I figured the competitor had reported me; regardless, I was fortunate enough to be able to talk myself out of a fine by telling them I was moving just a few things for a friend for free. They let me go, but it was a narrow escape.

I know I was a bit of a rebel in those days, but I have always justified it by insisting that was truly a matter of survival. On the other hand, I've never liked it when people tell me, "You can't do this or that." When I hear those words, I try to come up with a way to accomplish what I want.

You would think that my lack of license and proper insurance would have caused me to keep a low profile, and try my best to avoid drawing any official attention, but that wasn't the case. I was notorious for not paying parking tickets in Montreal. One night around 8 p.m., I heard a knock at my apartment door. When I opened it, I found two officers, who told me they had a warrant for my arrest. They claimed that I owed $300 in outstanding municipal parking tickets, and that unless I paid them immediately, they were taking me to jail. Being a bit of a joker, I quipped, "What, just the two of you?" They obviously didn't share my sense of humour, because they quickly retorted, "We can have four more officers here in minutes, if that's what it will take!" Not wanting trouble, I immediately went inside, got the money, and paid them. Then I wished them a good evening. From that point on, I was a little more careful about where I parked.

Murphy's law of "Whatever can go wrong will go wrong" must have been written for movers. Occasionally, I received calls from customers who had moving

jobs that were far beyond the capacity of my little
pickup truck. Since I never liked to turn down business,
I was inclined to put up a convincing front with potential customers. One incident involved a woman who
called about moving "a few rooms of furniture" from
the Town of Mount Royal to a location about 20 miles
away. I knew enough about Montreal neighbourhoods
to realize that houses in Mount Royal are usually large
and very expensive, with quality furniture. However, I
put on my selling cap and convinced the woman that I
could handle the job. I calculated that it would take me
three or four loads — to be frank, I had no idea how
many it might be. My rates were really low compared
to other movers, around $20 per hour for a truck and
two men. I guess this is what sold her, although I
explained I only had a small truck and would have to
make several trips.

My younger brother Ted was in town on vacation,
so I coerced him to give me a hand. When we arrived at
the address, we found ourselves in front of a mansion
with a driveway that would have accommodated a
dozen cars. Still undaunted, I rang the doorbell and a
man answered; perhaps it was the butler. He peered out
the giant wooden door and asked where the truck was,
and I sheepishly pointed to my tiny pickup. Let's just
say that he wasn't very impressed, but it was too late to
call another mover, so I entered the castle to see what
had to be moved.

You can imagine my shock when I was toured
through a 15-room house, which had at least 15,000 to
20,000 pounds of furniture needing to be moved.
That's a job for a 45-foot tractor-trailer, not a pickup
truck with an 8-foot box! In spite of the challenge

ahead of me, I set out to get the job done — or, at least, as much of it as I could, for the price quoted. It took us eight hours to move three loads of appliances and bedroom furniture, and since my brother was a novice mover, I was constantly explaining how things are done. One piece, in particular, was memorable: a huge credenza with thick sliding doors. I cautioned my brother to be careful, and to remember the doors. At our eventual destination, we had to carry it up a long flight of stairs. Ted went up backwards, and partway up, the heavy sliding doors came crashing down on my fingertips. Eventually, my nails turned black and fell off, which was a fitting end to the job I should never have accepted. Entrepreneurial drive is rarely fatal, but it can hurt. The rest of the furniture was eventually moved by another company who had a proper-sized moving van.

Operating a business without a license and insurance is almost a minor infraction compared to the next confession. As you know, I had no business training, and since I was running a one-man operation, I knew nothing about keeping proper records. Frankly, I was running it by the seat of my pants. To make matters worse (or better, depending on your definition), all my customers paid me in cash. This was the good old days, when real currency was still used even for larger purchases, and credit cards were only slowly making their existence felt. I think you can see where this is going: the truth is, I wasn't even filing tax returns! There it is in writing, and even after thirty years, this fact makes me shudder. However, all was not lost. Eventually, I met a chartered accountant — who later became my partner — who took on the task of bringing me up to date with the tax authorities and setting up some proper accounting systems. You can't imagine how relieved I was to have this issue settled, before I ended up in jail, and for something far more serious than unpaid parking tickets. And so, with the help of my future partner, I finally sorted out the issue of a proper operating license for a moving company.

My tendency to push the envelope has not been confined only to the moving business. It has entered some of my dealings with Premiere Executive Suites, which I began just over five years ago. I will explain more about Premiere in a later chapter but like my first moving company, it was started without a plan. I was a real novice at the accommodation business. I purchased a couple of condominiums and decided to rent them out. Before I knew it I owned ten condos and found myself trying to juggle all of the responsibilities of running a new business. This is when I decided I needed to put some structure around the new company. That being said, a number of situations arose that required me to reach back into my renegade past to deal with a couple of specific situations. As I've told you, sometimes I go around the rules, but in a way that can be rationalized or justified, thus usually not leading to any serious consequences. One example of this goes back to 1999, when I was just starting this company in Halifax. I had bought a residential townhouse on Bishop Street in downtown Halifax. It was a historic property, close to some commercial enterprises, and across from the Lieutenant Governor's Official Residence.

I had the idea of turning the main floor into Premiere's office, and creating extended stay accommodation units in the basement, as well as on the second and third floors. It seemed like an ideal setup to me. Sandra Bryant, one of the most successful realtors in the area, told me that she didn't think I could locate an office there, since the area was zoned as residential. This is not what I wanted to hear, so I didn't bother checking any further; I just went ahead and made a decision to do the renovations needed. It's the old "It's easier to beg for forgiveness than ask for permission" philosophy that I adhere to, when it suits my purposes. I soon created a highly attractive property, and the best part is that no one has ever questioned our right to have our offices in that location. We've since moved our offices three times due to our phenomenal growth.

I believe there is always a solution to any problem. Sometimes it just takes more effort to find it. Saying "no," to me, is an invitation to learning just how creative a problem solver I can become. I am a determined person, but I think I can honestly say that I haven't knowingly hurt anyone by any of my actions or decisions. I have little time for bureaucracy, and what I consider to be counter-productive rules. Usually, any projects I'm involved in provide an economic benefit, not just to me, but to the community where I am doing business. For example, in 2003 I decided to upgrade the Chester Business Centre, which I owned. It is located in the downtown section of our small town in Nova Scotia.

I have several tenants there, including Caldwell Banker Realty; Quirks, an arts and crafts shop; two Premiere accommodation units; and two apartments. I had a professional company come in, and build two kitchens and two bathrooms. The local building inspector called and asked how much I had spent. I told him it was around $15,000. He told me this was not a legal upgrade. Anything over $5,000 requires a permit. I apologized, and then asked him what he wanted me to do, take them out? He insisted on knowing who the contractor was, so he could go after him. I refused to provide him with this information. In retaliation, he put a stop-work order on my building. Fortunately for me, the work was complete by this time. Eventually, we worked things out. I didn't really have an issue with the regulations, I just resented the manner in which the inspector approached me. Rather than be professional, and try to work out a solution, he immediately went on the offensive. I responded in kind. My tenants appreciated the improvements I made, and they enhance the appearance and value of the real estate, which is good for the business community.

I will readily admit that I have made many decisions in my career that run contrary to normal business practices. I've taken risks — lots of them — but so have most successful entrepreneurs. That's what running a business is all about. There's no manual that tells you what to do in every conceivable situation. Sometimes you just have to go with your gut instinct. Whether you make a mental list of pros and cons (as I do) or you put pen to paper to make a formal list, either way you have to decide which way to go to get the result you want. Sometimes that means bending or even breaking the rules. As an entrepreneur, you will on occasion have to set aside your normal sense of caution and take a few risks for the sake of your company's future.

KEY LESSONS LEARNED

- When starting a business, sometimes you have to bend the rules to survive
- Be prepared to accept the consequences of your actions
- There is always a solution, even to what seems like an insurmountable problem

CHAPTER THREE

ENTREPRENEURS . . . BORN OR MADE?

"Success is the good fortune that comes from aspiration, desperation, perspiration, and inspiration."
— *Evan Escar*

There are some basic personality traits all entrepreneurs should possess in order to succeed. That being said, it is possible to develop and enhance these attributes over time, providing you are willing to work at it. Have a look at the following list and see if you recognize yourself in any or most of them:

PERSONAL ATTRIBUTES OF A SUCCESSFUL ENTREPRENEUR

- Self-Confidence
- Optimism/Positive Attitude/Enthusiasm
- Determination/Tenacity/Toughness
- Passion
- Self-Reliance
- A Strong Work Ethic
- Assertiveness
- An Ability to Motivate Others

- Integrity
- Respect for Others
- Humility
- Imagination

PROFESSIONAL ATTRIBUTES
- A Willingness to Take Risks
- A Sense of Urgency
- Communication Skills
- Vision
- Aptitude

Are you the type of employee who believes you have a responsibility to spend your employer's money wisely, to always give 110% to every task you perform, and to promote the company whenever you can? If so, you are already what business owners call an "intrapreneur." It is possible to think and act like an entrepreneur without actually owning part of the company, if this is what you choose to do. Smart employers will recognize your special qualities and they will reward you for your efforts.

Perhaps you yearn for something more, but still aren't sure if you are actually the entrepreneurial type or not. Here's another test:

- Are you the kind of employee who takes pride in doing a good job?
- Do you prefer to make your own decisions and find your own solutions to problems?
- Are you willing to be accountable for the results of your decisions?
- Do you want to make more money?

If the answer to these questions is yes, then it is quite likely entrepreneurship may be right for you. Perhaps all you need is the right opportunity and a little encouragement for you to take the next step into full-fledged entrepreneurship. The transition from employee to employer can be an exhilarating experience. The following saying is one I have always treasured: "Do what you love and you'll never have to work a day in your life." Those are words full of meaning to a successful entrepreneur.

Over the years, I have nurtured many intrapreneurs and helped them become entrepreneurs. One of the most dramatic examples is my former executive assistant, Kim Boydell, who left a secure nine-to-five job to become a partner in one of my business ventures, Premiere Executive Suites. Not only did she leave a good job, she took a 35% cut in salary — this, with two young children at home. Why would she do that, you ask? The answer is quite simple: Kim was finally ready to put her dreams into action — although, admittedly, she still had some reservations about her chances for success.

Was Kim a natural entrepreneur? Not by conventional standards. I can still recall my first few encounters with her. She was our sales secretary in the Toronto branch of my large, national moving company. I would see her during my daily walkabouts throughout the office. She was so shy and timid; she would hardly look at me, never mind speak to me. Therefore, when the time came for me to hire an executive assistant, Kim was the last person on my list of potential candidates. By contrast, her existing boss felt she deserved a promotion and would be a good choice. She typed 100 words per minute and had all of the necessary computer and administrative skills. I agreed she had the technical skills, but I was reluctant to hire her because I didn't think she had the right personality for the job. However, because of the high recommendation from her boss, I offered her the new position on a three-month trial basis. I figured this would be enough time for both of us to figure out if it would work or not, and it was in keeping with my practice of promoting from within, whenever possible.

From the beginning, Kim was very efficient. She came in around 7:30 a.m. and worked very hard. But one thing still bothered me. When I would call her each morning on my way in to the office, and asked her how she was, the answer was always the same: "Okay. How are you?" She just didn't come across in a particularly warm or friendly manner on the telephone, and frankly, this concerned me. I was afraid that she wouldn't make a good impression on the clients and business associates who called in to my office. I knew I had to address the problem, so I spoke to her about it. I explained why I felt it important for her to be more upbeat and enthusiastic, and I did my best to encourage her to see it my way. Things got a bit better, but I knew she had finally turned the corner when she sent an email to me that ended with the words, "Have a super day!"

Once in the position, Kim slowly changed and her personality became more outgoing. Before long, she mastered every task. This gave her more confidence, which in turn led to a willingness to start taking some initiative. During the next stage, she became comfortable making decisions on her own, and before long, she was working in a very intrapreneurial way. It was evident that the company's interests always came first with Kim. She became my "right-hand person," and one of my most trusted and appreciated employees. Kim was one of the best hiring decisions I have ever made. It was also apparent to me that she had a lot of potential, so I did my best to encourage and mentor her. I knew it was just a matter of time before she would be ready for an even greater challenge.

And I was right. Less than two years ago, she took a leap of faith, invested some of her own hard-earned money, and dove into the totally new world of owning her own business. If you were to ask her about her experiences, Kim would be quick to tell you that becoming an entrepreneur means being prepared to do whatever it takes to get your business off the ground and make it profitable. In her hospitality business (Premiere Executive Suites) this means doing a lot of menial jobs, especially in the beginning. Kim has spent hours making beds or hauling garbage off in her car so that her condos would be fresh and sparkling for the next guest. Kim will also tell you that becoming an entrepreneur was the right decision for her, albeit a scary one. Has it worked out for her? Most definitely. By her own admission, Kim genuinely looks forward to each new day. She feels revitalized, excited, and energetic. Her business is growing rapidly, and her net worth has increased tenfold. Her inspiring story and that of many others are recounted throughout this book, including a very special chapter, "Women in Power."

Like Kim, you will learn that to succeed, you will have to work harder than ever before, make more sacrifices, and take more risks. Everything else you can learn on the job, and from others who have gone before you.

You will have good periods and bad periods throughout your entrepreneurial career. There will be times when you will question why you ever wanted to start your own business with all of the demands and challenges that come with the territory. This is when your faith in yourself and in your decision to become an entrepreneur must remain steadfast. Being able to remain positive and confident during these difficult times is the difference between success and failure.

I once read a quote by Katherine Mansfield related to positive thinking that stuck with me: "I have made a rule in my life never to regret and never to look back. Regret is an appalling waste of energy . . . you can't build on it; it's only good for wallowing in." A positive outlook is the one essential ingredient that every entrepreneur must have. Being in business for yourself is no fun if you allow yourself to think disaster is just around the corner. That's not to say that having a positive attitude will keep problems away, but it will help you deal with them and then move on to better things. Believing in yourself is essential if you want to be a successful entrepreneur. If you don't believe in yourself, then how could you ever expect others to do so?

As I mentioned at the beginning of this chapter, there are a number of traits and attributes common to most successful entrepreneurs. I'd like to expand on some of them and offer a few suggestions as to things you can do to maximize their effectiveness.

Self-Confidence

If you want to be a successful entrepreneur, *you must look, sound, and act in a confident manner at all times.*

As a fledgling entrepreneur, it is only natural to be nervous, but you can't let it show. I'd like to give you a few suggestions on how to project an air of confidence to everyone you meet. At first glance, these suggestions may seem simple and obvious, but you would be surprised at how many people fail at the basics when it comes to appearing confident. This is particularly true if they are making the transition from worker to entrepreneur within the same industry. Too often, people don't adjust their appearance, speech, or approach to a manner befitting that of a business owner. Consequently, neither customers nor employees take them seriously. Here are some of my key recommendations:

- Dress for Success . . . Invest in top quality clothing
- Develop a Strong Handshake . . . It is an extension of your image
- Use Voice Modulation to Your Advantage . . . You will appear in control
- Improve Your Vocabulary . . . You will appear better educated
- Practise Good Manners . . . "Please" and "Thank you" *never* go out of style

The concepts listed above may be second nature to you, but I can tell you that when I went from being the owner of a small, local moving company to my second entrepreneurial venture as the co-owner of a nationally affiliated one, I had to make an effort to put them into practice on a daily basis. Up until that point, I was virtually a one man show, doing everything from sales to working on the trucks. I lived in my mover's uniform, and dealt only with the homeowners who were moving.

In my new incarnation, I was required to meet corporate clients, van line executives, and other business types, and convince them I was capable of running this new, more complex business. Taking clients to lunch or making presentations was a foreign world to me. I owned one suit, didn't even have a credit card, and my level of confidence was non-existent.

I can still recall my sense of fear, but I made sure that I did not let this show when dealing with these people. If I had revealed any sign of weakness or lack of confidence, my newfound associates would have immediately dismissed me as being unworthy to be a member of their team. The only person who really knew how inadequate I felt was my wife. I remember saying to her, "I don't know if I can do this!" Loyal spouse that she was, Bernardine generously replied, "Oh, of course you can." Thankfully, she was right.

Optimism/Positive Attitude/Enthusiasm

In my experience, an *entrepreneur must first and foremost have an optimistic and positive outlook on life.* The ability to see the glass half-full will help you get through the tough times. A positive attitude and an enthusiastic demeanour are also good for your business, because these traits are infectious. They attract people; employees want to work with you, customers want to do business with you. It's important to create a sense of excitement around your business. It creates positive energy. When you are excited, those around you become excited. It's really quite startling to see this in practice. If you can accomplish this, you will be on your way to creating a great corporate culture.

In contrast, people who have a negative outlook on life generally don't make good entrepreneurs. Their cynicism, sarcasm, and fear of the future drive people away. If you are trying to decide if running your own business is a viable option for you, I'd recommend that you be brutally honest with yourself about the issue of attitude. The same is true when assessing potential employees. If they have a positive attitude and are enthusiastic about the job, they can usually be trained and molded. On the other hand, all the skills in the world won't make up for a bad attitude in someone.

Determination/Tenacity/Toughness

Determination, tenacity, and toughness are also essential to surviving and succeeding in business. Specifically, it means you:

- Have the ability to make the difficult decisions when necessary
- Refuse to give up when faced with adversity
- Don't let people take advantage of you or abuse you
- Keep trying to achieve your goals, even if you fail the first, or first few, times
- Find alternative solutions to problems
- Refuse to accept "no" for an answer
- Always ask for more than you expect to receive
- Understand there is always a solution to a problem — you just have to *find* it

Growing up, I witnessed firsthand why talent was *not* enough to be successful in business. My father was a great salesman but not a great businessman. He worked hard and people loved him, but he just didn't have the necessary degree of determination and toughness to really make a success out of his business. He allowed people to take advantage of him, and he failed to act when it was in his best interest. For example, he didn't fire one employee who stole from him, he didn't chase after people who owed him money, and he was too easy on employees who didn't work hard enough. To make matters worse, my father insisted on living beyond our family's means. In spite of these failings, he managed to hang on to his business for 30 years before twice going bankrupt. Those financial pressures were hard on our family, and eventually led to my parents' divorce. While I didn't realize it at the time, I guess I learned a lesson from my father's experiences that I was able to use when I tried my hand at being an entrepreneur, and for that, I will always be grateful to him.

Passion

I realize the word passion is somewhat overused in today's parlance, but frankly, there really isn't a better word to describe the way you should feel about your business. *Entrepreneurs who love what they do are more likely to be successful.* Sometimes just being in business for yourself is enough to arouse that passion. However, if you can find a type of business that is compatible with your personal interests, then that is a bonus. Think about it: What type of work environment would make you happiest? Don't just focus on your past work experience. Open yourself up to some other possibilities. If you really like dealing with people, chances are you will gravitate towards a service type of business, as I did. Now that you are contemplating going out on your own, make it the kind of business that will have you jumping out of bed each morning, excited and energized to see what each day will bring. It's quite simple, really; if you like what you do, you'll be better at it.

I remember making a presentation to a senior banker and I was so enthused that after about 15 minutes, he said, "You really love what you do." I agreed, and to this day I think that my passion for my company was so overwhelming I made a believer out of him, and he in turn entrusted his business to us. Never underrate the value of being passionate about your company.

I must admit that the foregoing advice represents the ideal situation. Sometimes that perfect opportunity just isn't on the horizon. That's when it's important to look at alternatives. Find something where the pros outweigh the cons. When I decided to go into the moving business, I didn't choose it because I liked lifting furniture or driving a truck. (I often joke that "No child tells their parents they want to be a professional mover when they grow up!") I did it because it gave me a chance to be my own boss and to make more money than I could make working as a teacher. There were aspects of the work that I didn't like, but the positives outweighed the negatives. By the time I owned my second, much larger moving company, my passion was still less about the actual business of moving and more about the challenge of creating a national multi-branch company that specialized in corporate employee relocations. How we performed made a difference in the lives of the families who were entrusted to our care.

And over the years, I discovered that I had a genuine ability to inspire and motivate others, which added another dimension to my passion for my work. Today, one of my greatest joys in life comes from helping ignite that same passion in other aspiring or fledgling entrepreneurs.

Communication Skills

Of all the entrepreneurial skills being discussed in this chapter, communication is one of the most important. It is also one that can be learned. The ability to communicate and deal with people is essential to running a business. I recently read an article about a study that was done involving MBA students. The study found that while these individuals had exceptional qualitative and quantitative skills, most were seriously lacking in basic interpersonal skills. The students' employers, interviewed in the study, saw this as an area in need of serious improvement. *Your ability to be an effective communicator is crucial to your overall business success.*

Your employees are made up of a broad range of people, all of whom have their own diverse personalities, values, and agendas. You must learn to adapt your communication style to match each member of this important group. Doing this leads to communication that is more effective.

I've always been a believer in a "straight line" type of management structure. As far as I am concerned, titles are only there for external use (with clients, bankers, and others). I am no different than any other employee in the company. We are all there to do a job, be professional, and pay our way. Frontline employees are especially important in an organization because they interface with the customer first.

Employees, whatever their level, must be treated with respect. You must also demonstrate a genuine interest in them as individuals. For example, with my Premiere Executive Suites business, I make sure that I get to know all of the housekeeping and maintenance staff. These employees are on duty every day, cleaning and caring for our condominiums and inns. Our guests' level of satisfaction is tied directly to the quality of the work done by the employees. If our staff members feel appreciated, they do a better job, are friendlier to the guests, and generally present the kind of image we want for our properties.

I followed the same principle with my two moving companies. There, it was our drivers and packers who were in a position to make or break our reputation for service. I encouraged them to stop by anytime they were in the office. I wanted to know them and let them know me. I was even willing to let them talk me into arm-wrestling contests. Silly as that may sound, it created a unique bond between us. Every minute spent with my frontline service providers was time well spent. They learned to trust, respect, and like me, which was good for the company. They knew I cared about them, and in turn, they made a real effort to do an outstanding job for our customers. It was a real win/win situation for all stakeholders in the company.

The same advice applies to anyone you come in contact with throughout the course of your day. I've made it a point to be nice to everyone I meet, regardless of his or her position. As an example, there is a parking lot at the corner of Front and York Streets in Toronto that I frequent. It's a very busy place. Over the years, I've gotten to know two of the parking lot attendants simply by making casual conversation with them. Because I don't act like they are invisible, I stand out among their many customers. As a result, whenever I pull in they always find a spot for me even if the "lot full" sign is on. It feels good to be nice to people on a purely human level, and sometimes it even has its own rewards.

I've been told my ability to communicate with people is one of my greatest strengths. Here are a few tips that have worked for me, with both employees and customers:

- Have an open door policy; be accessible
- Ensure that employees know they can approach you to discuss problems without fear of consequences or retribution
- Be honest and up-front with them, even when discussing sensitive matters
- Listen to their ideas and opinions
- Show a sincere interest in people and their lives outside work
- Be honourable. Keep your promises

Communicating with employees on a regular basis is an important part of managing your business and is well worth the time it may take out of your busy schedule. Part of my regular routine in my moving business was to walk about the office, stopping to chat with as many of my employees as possible. At the time, we probably had about 90 people working in the Toronto location. I did the same whenever I travelled to our various branch locations. I now continue the practice at all of our Premiere Executive Suites offices across the country. It's amazing how much information I pick up, since this is a very non-threatening form of communication. The employees feel special, because they see I am interested in them as individuals. At the same time, their self-esteem is enhanced, because they quickly realize I'm no different from anyone else in the company. I have challenges and personal problems, just as they do. These informal chats strengthen the bond between us, which makes for a better employer/employee relationship.

I always make sure to thank people for their efforts. It certainly doesn't cost anything, but it is most definitely appreciated. I'm constantly amazed that more employers and bosses don't do this. Far too many keep themselves totally remote from their employees, unless of course they are taking them to task about something. I can tell you from decades of experience that it is easier to deliver constructive criticism or bad news to people if they like and respect you. I've never wanted any employee to fear me. Personally, I feel this is a counterproductive way to run a company. If you take only a single piece of advice away from this book, make it *communicate with and get to know your employees.* Talk to them on their level. If you need a reason, just remember that you'll reap rewards in the form of loyalty and productivity, and keeping good employees saves your company money. The near total lack of turnover in each of the businesses I've created since the 1970s underlines the truth of this statement.

Humility

At first glance, this may seem like a strange attribute to be promoting, but I can tell you endless stories about entrepreneurs who became successful and then saw that success diminish as a result of their inability to remember where they came from.

People will applaud your achievements as long as you don't become arrogant. Few businesses succeed simply because of the efforts of just one person. It takes a committed, dedicated team of talented people to help a business grow and prosper. One of the biggest mistakes entrepreneurs can make is to start believing they did it solely on their own. *Acknowledge the contributions of others, and make sure you thank them as often as you can.* Introduce your team members to important customers, or to any visitors who drop by your place of business, to let them know your company has "bench strength," as they say in sports. It will give your clients even more confidence in your company's ability to be of service to them.

Don't become remote from your employees and customers. The minute you start thinking you are superior, you will get into trouble. Once you isolate yourself from what is happening on a daily basis, you begin to lose touch with your business. Problems may be occurring behind the scenes, and you certainly do not want to be the last to know about them. You should never be too busy or feel too important to take the time to talk to employees, or even deal with irate customers. People like to deal with the person at the top, and why shouldn't they? Your direct involvement can often save the company's reputation in the event a serious situation arises. Like anything else in life, practice makes perfect. The foregoing attributes can be developed and enhanced over time. As an entrepreneur, you must make an effort to use all of your talents. Identify your shortcomings and then work hard to improve them. The real trick is to do this on a consistent basis. It takes concentration and focus but I can assure you it's worth it. Each little success experienced will build upon previous successes and before you know it, you will feel strong and confident about your ability as an entrepreneur.

KEY LESSONS LEARNED

- Many successful entrepreneurs share similar attributes
- Intrapreneurial employees are valuable to their employers
- When they are (finally) ready, intrapreneurs *can* become entrepreneurs
- Entrepreneurial attributes are a combination of natural and learned behaviours
- Focus and practice will help improve your entrepreneurial skills

CHAPTER FOUR

BREAKING NEW GROUND

"It takes courage to push yourself to places you've never been . . . to test your limits . . . to break through barriers."
— *Anais Nin*

With a group of hard-working, dedicated partners and employees, I spent 22 years creating the largest, most successful moving company in the country. When AMJ Campbell Van Lines was founded in 1977, there were several large national moving company groups already operating in Canada. These firms were well established and well known. When we came on the scene, these groups viewed us as an upstart and a minor competitor. That attitude changed very quickly once we started to take business away from the "big boys." We managed to out-service, outsell, and outwit our competitors. No one ever dreamed we would become Canada's best-known moving company, but we did!

I think there is useful information about our specific company that may benefit other organizations. There are some valuable lessons to be learned from studying our journey, which took us from two small offices in a single province to 46 major locations stretched from the Atlantic to the Pacific oceans. Sales went from $250,000 in 1977 to $125 million within two decades. To understand how we ended up where we did, you need to know a little bit about where we started. For that reason, I'd like to take you back to 1977 and then move forward, recounting some of the major milestones and challenges along the way.

When I sold TC Moore Transport, my first, Montreal-based moving company, I intended to go back to teaching. I had several offers, and was in the process of deciding which one I would accept. However, fate intervened, in the form of an opportunity that was too good to refuse. My former accountant from Montreal approached me in 1977 about becoming his partner in a moving company that had two small offices in Barrie and Toronto, Ontario. The company was called MJ Campbell Moving and Storage, and had annual sales of $250,000. It had been in business for over 40 years, but the current owners were having some financial difficulties and were looking to sell. He explained to me that the company had tremendous potential because it was an agent for North American Van Lines. This affiliation meant it was in a legal position to do moving throughout Canada and the United States. It also had a contractual arrangement to handle moves for the Department of National Defense's large army base near Barrie. And, having an office in Toronto would allow us to take advantage of the booming corporate relocation market.

I quickly decided that I was definitely interested in becoming involved in this venture. I knew from my earlier experience with TC Moore that there was good money to be made in the moving business, especially if you were able to service the long-distance side of the business. MJ Campbell had a proper operating authority for interprovincial moving so this would be a big step up from the type of renegade operation I had run in Montreal. No more midnight driver, dodging scale masters along highway 401. I decided that my return to the classroom could wait a little longer. I figured it wouldn't be forever, since our plan was to build up the business over 3 or 4 years, and then sell it for a profit. That would give me a bit of a nest egg, and then I could return to teaching, free of financial worries. Little did I know that I was embarking on a journey that would see a 4-year plan stretch to 22 years.

Needless to say, I didn't fully realize what I was getting into. Operating MJ Campbell was far more complex than anything I had done to date. But I did have some good instincts. In spite of receiving a D in marketing at university, I came up with a number of good ideas to help promote the company. The first thing I did was change the firm's name from MJ Campbell Moving and Storage to AMJ Campbell Van Lines. This automatically gave the company a more prominent position at the front of the mover's section in the Yellow Pages. By this time, I realized that 70% to 80% of most moving business comes from Yellow Page advertising so I understood the value of moving to the front of the book. Adding the term "van lines" instead of the usual "moving and storage" gave a national flavour to our identity. I also thought this would help us sell to the corporate market. Because we were already affiliated with North American Van Lines, I was effectively creating a "van line within a van line" type of structure for our company. This alone made us stand out from the competition. Being part of North American was important because it gave us access to their massive resources, including a large hauling fleet and agent representatives all over North America.

Once we had a new name, I decided to create an image for the company. This extended to every facet of our business, from our distinctive logo to our drivers in full uniforms (including ties — something that had never been done before or since). I was determined to make us stand out in a crowded marketplace.

Now that I was operating a much larger company, I started looking for ways to maximize profitability. One area that drew my attention was that of driver and packer compensation packages. Most companies paid these people by the hour, but I felt this was a disincentive to productivity. We wanted our service providers to be more entrepreneurial, so we decided to pay them a percentage of the revenue from each job they worked on. We also made them more accountable for their performance, which included making them partially responsible for the cost of any damage claims. A claim-free or low-claim move meant that everyone made more money. At the same time we developed a bonus program to reward them for a job well done. Once our people got used to the new system, they found they were actually making more money. They began to take more pride in how they did their job. Customers who had moved previously realized the quality of our service was at a higher level than they had experienced with other movers. Word got around and we gradually became the mover of choice for many of Canada's largest corporations.

I believe one of the best ways to get managers and

senior employees to go above and beyond the call of duty is to let them buy shares in the company. This is what I did at AMJ Campbell. When people have a vested interest, they work harder and pay more attention to the way they spend the company's money. The secret to selling shares is to make the cost very affordable for your employees. Offering the option of an installment plan or co-signing for a loan is another way to help employees to make the investment. Next, I turned my attention to business development. Already I was dreaming about expansion, but I knew this was out of the question until the company was on solid financial ground. In order to accomplish my plan, I knew I had to hire outstanding salespeople.

One of the first people I hired was a corporate salesman by the name of Ron Stone. As a former van line executive, he understood all aspects of the business. Ron was experienced, presentable, and personable. He had all the right attributes to be a successful corporate salesman. Even better, he was willing to help me get acclimatized to my new world. We would go out together on sales calls, and I would tell clients about my wild and crazy days as a local mover in Montreal. (The "broom story" always got a few laughs.) Then, Ron would handle the formal presentation part of the sales call, explaining why the corporation should trust their employee relocations to us. His polish and my enthusiasm made a positive impression on potential clients.

I came to believe that *working in tandem with another salesperson can be one of the most effective ways to develop new business.* I still do this whenever I can, and I recommend that you try it in your business and see if it makes a difference. The secret lies in selecting the right pair of individuals. Each should bring complementary strengths to the process. It's been my experience that it can be very effective when a man and a woman work together as a team. Each gender has special attributes, and together they can create exactly the right balance for a sales presentation.

By late 1980, the company was doing well, and we had already expanded into Ottawa, Montreal, Edmonton, Calgary, and Vancouver. I had even convinced my brother Terry to give up his secure sales manager's job with Phillips Electronics to open our Western offices. When our sales reached $3 million (a tenfold increase over where we started), I remember asking myself and others, "How much more can we grow?" Herein lies yet another lesson for aspiring entrepreneurs: *Never put any limits on yourself or your company.* Anything is possible, if you want it badly enough, and are willing to work for it. It was then that I made one of the boldest moves of my entire career.

By the time I had been running the business for about three years, I realized that this was what I wanted to do with my life. I enjoyed the challenges involved in being an entrepreneur. I was also young, aggressive, and hungry for more business. We had already achieved a fair measure of success but I knew that there were even brighter times ahead, providing I could continue to bring outstanding people into the company. I decided to start my search within the hallowed halls of North American Van Lines' own subsidiary companies. I knew that their employees were the best trained and the most successful salespeople in the industry. I set my sights on the very best person working for the organization. Here I was, the new kid on the North American block, and I had the audacity to try to recruit Jacqueline Stewart, the top salesperson in the entire moving industry. Obviously, the management at North American wasn't happy about this when they got wind of my plans. Jackie was a legend, first because of her phenomenal sales performance (more than $1.5 million per year), and second because she was known as the nicest, classiest woman in the business. Everyone loved and admired her.

Now, I must admit Jackie did not jump at the opportunity. It took a lot of persuading to get her to leave her very lucrative job. She eventually joined us in 1981 and from that point forward, our company got the attention and respect that I desired. Jackie gave us instant credibility. With someone of her calibre on board, the company started moving full steam ahead, acquiring new corporate clients at a head-turning pace. I tell this story because there is a very important lesson contained within: *If you want to be a huge success, you must have the best people working with you. Don't settle for ordinary performers, go after the superstars.* Whatever business you get into, you should find out who are the top salespeople in that industry, and you should go after them with everything you have.

To get the best, you have to be prepared to pay them what they are worth. You also have to sell yourself and make them want to work with you. Hiring the right people is a two-way street. Top performers don't change employers without a good reason. That's why you must do your utmost to convince them that your company is right for them. Obviously you believe in your company, but you have to make believers out of prospective employees. People of this calibre can have their pick of jobs, so when you spot someone you want in your organization, treat them like a customer. Do your best to sell them on your company.

You will find that success breeds success, as the old saying goes. AMJ Campbell was so different from anyone else in the industry, and our ambition knew no bounds. I go into more detail in another chapter on how to stand out from the crowd, but, in brief, it was our people, our creative marketing programs, our value-added benefits, and our determination to be the biggest and the best that set us apart. With each new branch that opened and each new top-quality person added, our reputation grew exponentially.

In 1984, we made moving industry history for two reasons. First, we purchased four acres of prime property in the heart of Mississauga, Ontario. It was here that we built a showcase building. Our 100,000-square-foot office/warehouse complex was as far from the typical mover's premises as you could get. Second, by late 1984, our relationship with North American Van Lines had seriously deteriorated. We felt they were in a serious conflict of interest with their subsidiary company offices and their own hauling fleet. This is when we started negotiating with Atlas Van Lines, who were the smallest van line in the industry at the time.

The deal we struck with Atlas, which included a $1 million signing bonus and $500,000 in conversion costs, was unprecedented and got the attention of our competitors. The lesson here is that sometimes it makes the most sense to be a huge fish in a small pond than a small fish in a big pond. Taking our company out of North American was a bold step. It could have backfired on us . . . but didn't. In fact, it turned into a good news story for both AMJ and Atlas as we grew and prospered together. In 1988, we attracted the attention of a venture capital group, Vector, that was comprised of a number of high profile individuals, including John Tory, Former Chief Justice Willard Estey, and Senator Michael Meehan. They saw us as a good investment and made an offer to purchase 70% of the company based on a value of $10.5 million. Each share was valued at $110,000. Our managers and senior employees who had bought shares got a big payday. Needless to say, everyone was thrilled. We retained 30% ownership and the day-to-day responsibility for running the company. A year later we bought out one of our competitors, CP Moving, which was owned by Canadian Pacific Enterprises. Atlas contributed to the cost of this acquisition. By 1990, our company had become a household name, outshining other companies that had been around for nearly a century. It was a truly exhilarating experience for anyone involved in our firm.

Times were good until the recession of the early 1990s. In another chapter, I go into a bit more detail about the tough times but in concise terms, it was a time of belt tightening for the company. I was determined that we would not be one of the casualties of the recession. This meant that we had to be lean and mean during this downturn in the economy. I'm proud to say that we came out of those dark days with 19% growth in revenues, and a phenomenal 30% growth in our bottom line. It was also during this period that we started to franchise many of our company-owned branches. I attribute our ability to weather a serious recession in part to our people. They made sacrifices for the good of the company, and worked even harder through these tough times. They believed in the company and in each other. Most of them subscribed to the philosophy that "tough times don't last but tough people do." I will always be grateful to the many individuals who rallied to the cause.

Then in 1992 our parent company, Vector, decided to take the company public on the Toronto Stock Exchange (under the name of CAMVEC) in an effort to increase the value of the company. A new chairman was installed to help manage the company. By 1996 the company was back in a healthy financial position with $5 million in the bank and no debt. This was a good news/ bad news story for the company.

The good news was that we had weathered the recession far better than any of our competitors. The bad news was that our chairman, Arthur Walker, was anxious to spend some of that $5 million on another acquisition. He convinced his board of directors to let him pursue this avenue. The acquisition would have been successful if he had chosen a business that was more synergistic with our own, but instead he went totally outside the company's area of expertise and invested in a horticulture product company, Kord Products. This was a disastrous acquisition and was the beginning of more tough times for AMJ, which struggled each year, losing more and more money on Kord. By 1999, the chairman was projecting a loss of $3 million on Kord. The actual loss was closer to $20 million. Earlier in the year I had decided to step out of the grind of daily management and had taken on the role of advisory chairman. Most of my time was spent in Halifax while all this was going on, and since AMJ was now a public company, I was no longer in a position to make any decisions relating to Kord. CAMVEC's chairman and his board of directors were in the driver's seat.

This story is important because it shows you what can happen when you sell a majority stake in your company to a third party. The upside is you usually reap a huge financial return. The downside is you end up losing control. You have to be cognizant of this fact when you make your decision to sell. In retrospect, I think we may have been better off to retain full ownership of the company. I'm sure that if we had, any acquisition we would have chosen to make would have been more complementary to our core business. But as they say, hindsight is 20/20.

My opposition to some of what was going on at the company and some personal issues with the new management led to my departure in 1999. A few more details on this subject are included in chapter 13, "Lessons Learned the Hard Way." In 2003, the company had to fight off an attempted hostile takeover. To do this, they had to find a white knight, thus saddling the firm with significant debt. Other issues, including the departure of a large number of senior people, several messy lawsuits, and growing disenchantment on the part of 17 franchisees, have all impacted negatively on the company. In April 2005, this group of franchisees broke away from AMJ and joined me in my new venture, Premiere Van Lines.

Even the most successful company can lose its way when it stops paying attention to the people who helped make it great. No matter what pressures a company finds itself burdened with, it is imperative for management to stay focused on the people and the day-to-day operation of the business.

KEY LESSONS LEARNED

- Expand to multiple locations to grow your company
- Make your company unique and differentiated from the competition
- Hire the best people possible — even look outside your industry to find them
- Try team selling — it works!
- Resist the urge to acquire non-synergistic businesses, unless you have an exceptional operator
- Remember: too much debt is deadly
- Don't mess with a winning formula

CHAPTER FIVE

EXPANDING YOUR HORIZONS

"If a window of opportunity appears, don't pull down the shade."
— *Tom Peters*

True entrepreneurs thrive on challenges. Rarely are they satisfied with the status quo. When they achieve a measure of success, generally that makes them hungry for more. It's been that way for me and for many other successful businesspeople I have met over the years. I have always been a proponent of growing a business by expanding its reach on a national or international basis. This way, you can maximize your market potential in each region. If you are just starting out as an entrepreneur, then the idea of expansion may be the last thing on your mind. However, if you are like me, it won't be long before you start thinking about opening another branch or franchise. The Golden Rule to abide by concerning expansion is: ***Don't even think about expanding until you make a success of your first operation.***

My mind is always two or three steps ahead of my current situation. Over the years, I have developed an innate sense of when the time is right to start thinking about expansion. For example, one day I was visiting Premiere Executive Suites' Montreal office while my partner/manager for the branch, Tatiana Kredl, was in Toronto. The office is located in a historic house on Lakeshore Road in Dorval. We spent a lot of time and money renovating this building without destroying its character and charm. In addition to our office, we had four guest suites. I was enjoying the comforts of Tatiana's beautifully decorated office when it suddenly occurred to me that since we had a large piece of property with lots of room for parking, it would make sense to expand our business by adding three new units on to the back of the building. We had only been in business in Montreal for a short time, but things were going very well. The more I thought about it, the more excited I got. I figured we could sell one of our other condos in the city and take the $60,000 that we would realize on the sale and put it towards the cost of constructing the new units. Not wanting to wait a minute longer, I got on the phone to our contractor. He gave me a ballpark estimate of $200,000 for the work. I was feeling very pleased with myself for having come up with this idea.

No sooner did I hang up from talking to the contractor than the telephone rang. It was Tatiana calling from Toronto. I knew she really loved her office. She considered it her "home away from home" and was kind enough to let me use it while she was out of town. Since we are good friends and have a great rapport, I was in the mood to tease her a little. "I really like this office, Tatiana. You know, I'm getting really used to it." I could sense she was getting a little flustered since she wasn't sure where I was going with my comments. It's possible that she thought I was planning to move in and take over her office. I decided it was time to stop teasing and tell her about my brainstorm. Much to my surprise, she wasn't quite as excited as I was about the plan to expand.

After our discussion, I realized she was just nervous about how fast I was moving to expand our Montreal operation. Once she gave it some serious thought, she agreed it made a lot of sense. We went ahead with the expansion and it has dramatically improved the profitability of this location. At the time, Tatiana was a relatively new entrepreneur — only two years in her exciting new role — and was still a little cautious. Since then we have grown the business considerably and Tatiana has developed her own sense of when the time is right to expand into new projects.

There is one cautionary note about expansion that I must emphasize. You must be in a strong cash position before you contemplate opening any new locations. Expanding too quickly has been the downfall of many companies in this country. Don't try to expand too rapidly using borrowed money. If you've been making good profits and feel the time is right to buy new equipment or open new branches, then use that money to carry out your plans. Many savvy businesspeople make the mistake of thinking that bigger is always better. That's not always the case, especially if you don't have the financial resources to handle the cost of expansion. I'll give you a couple of examples.

In 1988, Vector purchased 70% of my national moving company, AMJ Campbell Van Lines, based on a value of $10.5 million. Our company was known to be an aggressive, growth-oriented organization with strong management and good profitability. Vector decided they would continue to allow us to make our own decisions about future expansion, since we had managed this area quite well in the past. The second company they bought into was another story. Vector spent $17 million to buy A&A Records. Within one year, they opened 100 new stores. Unfortunately, they had neither the financial foundation nor the right store operators to handle this level of expansion. Consequently, A&A Records declared bankruptcy and all Vector members lost a significant amount of money.

Another example of expanding too soon involved one of my own moving company franchisees, who had a marginally successful business in London, Ontario. Rather than turn things around in London, he borrowed more money so he could expand into Windsor and go into the freight business (which he knew nothing about). This approach only made things worse. Eventually he managed to improve his situation, but it was a long, hard road back to solvency.

Many entrepreneurs get into trouble because they let debt build up until it becomes unmanageable. I have always made it a practice to pay off loans or mortgages as quickly as possible. I've never expanded my business unless I could afford to do so. From my initial $2,000 loan from the bank of Montreal to buy my pickup truck, to the hundreds of loans and mortgages taken out over the years to expand my business or invest in real estate, my approach has remained the same: Borrow only what you need and accelerate payment. The result for me is a stellar credit rating, which gives me easier access to funds whenever I have a new project.

Banks are generally very conservative when it comes to small-business loans. In Canada, banks are often viewed as being inflexible, which makes it difficult for some entrepreneurs to get their businesses up and running. This is why it's imperative for you to establish a relationship with your banker. You can't just be a name on a loan or line of credit application. Although most bankers are tied to pre-set formulas for granting credit, it still helps if they at least know who you are and what you are trying to accomplish with your business. I've always approached banks the way I approach customers. I want them to believe in my companies or projects and their potential. I work hard to get them excited about my business. If you do this too, you will find that dealing with your banker will be a far less intimidating experience.

I've made it a practice that all new mortgages for Premiere Executive Suites, regardless of size, have a shorter than normal amortization period. In fact, the first 28 mortgages I took out for Premiere were all amortized over a 12-year period, which is virtually unheard of with a start-up operation. My bankers know my philosophy and they know how I feel about debt, so they are always willing to work with me. For example, I have a $1.8 million line of credit at prime with a major bank. Several times a year I get together with my banker to tell him what I am doing, what I anticipate my borrowing requirements will be, what significant cheques will be going through, and where I expect my bank position to be over the next four to six months. This practice gives my banker a sense of confidence about how I am conducting my business dealings. I'm proud of my ability to maintain a good working relationship with bankers in various parts of the country.

To keep this kind of relationship going, you have to

stay in contact with your banker. Many entrepreneurs go out of their way to avoid talking to the banking officer. A meeting at the bank is viewed with as much enthusiasm as going for a root canal at the dentist. I take the opposite approach and look for opportunities to call my banker to talk about what's going on in the company, what new accounts we've acquired or are working on, who we've recently hired, or any other information I think will present the company in a good light. Doing this definitely takes my banking transactions out of the realm of a name on a file. We become real people doing good work, and bankers feel more confident about our prospects. When the time comes to expand, they have a good sense of how we conduct ourselves and are usually more willing to help us. Communicating with your banker is even more important whenever you find yourself in a bit of a bind. At times like that, it really helps if your banker knows and believes in you. If they do, they will work with you, providing you are totally honest with them and have a plan to turn things around.

As well as managing debt, all entrepreneurs need to know where they stand financially, at all times. I always watched my companies' expenses to ensure we didn't get too far into our line of credit unless it was necessary, and even then I made sure we paid it down as quickly as possible. I would recommend that as an entrepreneur you get in the habit of signing all your company cheques. That way, you will always have a good sense of where your money is going and if it is being spent wisely. I call my business partners regularly to ask them about their bank position, their receivables, their revenues, and their profit. I like to have this information available since it gives me a good indication of how we are doing at all times. If you are running a business, you need to know where you stand on a daily, or at least a weekly, basis.

Managing your money wisely will allow you to expand when the right opportunity comes along. As I've already told you, I rarely have detailed, long-term plans drawn up in advance. My approach to business is directed to a major degree based on gut instinct. I have to admit that today I am in the fortunate position of being able to afford it, should things not work out. Obviously, I was more cautious in my early days, but making sure I am on solid financial ground before expanding is the one rule from which I have never deviated. At the same time, I've always relied on my instinct to help me make a quick decision rather than let a good opportunity get away. Interestingly enough, some of the world's most successful entrepreneurs, including Donald Trump and Sir Richard Branson, do this as well. As you mature as an entrepreneur, you will learn to trust those instincts.

I'll give you an example of not having a plan that worked out well. A few years ago, I was visiting Moncton, New Brunswick, when I saw a lovely historic house that I just fell in love with — so I bought it. I figured I would do some renovations and make it a Premiere Executive Suites property. Shortly after the purchase, I was chatting with my former executive assistant and she asked me if I had done a market study to determine if Moncton would be a good location for Premiere. I said, "Yes, I did the same market study for Moncton that I did when I started in Halifax." In other words . . . none. I knew there was a market there, I just didn't know how large it was, but I was willing to take a calculated risk.

I don't want you to think that I blindly go off and open new locations without giving it some thought. But I also don't spend endless hours analyzing market potential or reading charts or checking out statistical data. In my opinion, many people miss out on good business opportunities because they spend too much time analyzing and re-analyzing — what's referred to as "analysis paralysis." In business, you have to learn to make decisions quickly. It's the old 80/20 rule that applies to many things in life: if you make the right decision 80% of the time, then you will have a good success ratio. The real key is to *develop the ability to make a decision.* Over time, most good entrepreneurs will start to trust their own instincts after they have a few successes under their belt.

My two main business interests, moving (AMJ Campbell Van Lines, 1977–1999) and extended-stay accommodations (Premiere Executive Suites, 1999–present) have some natural synergies. Both businesses cater to people who relocate, accept work assignments in a new location, or travel on business. Therefore, we can cross-market our services to the same clientele. From a market research point of view, the questions that need to be answered for either business are quite basic. Depending on the nature of your business, I'm sure you could come up with equally simple questions. In my case, I ask:

1. Is there a reasonable number of people in the area who would be in need of our services?
2. Are there any corporations based in the area? (People

are often relocated in or out)

3. Is there a relatively healthy real estate market in the area? (People always need to move)
4. Are there any hotels in the area? (People need a place to stay)
5. Is the area accessible by road, rail, or air?
6. Is the area growing and economically viable?
7. Is there competition in the area? (Competition is good! It means there is a market)

If I like the answers, I move on to the next step, which is finding *a superb operator for the location.* This individual must be someone who has already achieved a high degree of success in their career. It's a bonus if they have experience in my business, but it's not imperative; just as long as they have the right attitude and the right skill set. They must also fit into our corporate culture. My final criteria is that operators be prepared to invest some of their own money to become an equity partner. The equity percentage can vary depending on the circumstances, but generally it's between 15 and 25% to start. Often, we offer an option to purchase shares over a specific period.

The issue of *fitting in with the existing corporate culture is critical.* If you open locations across the country, you want the operator of each location to get along with their peers in other cities. If you have the right people as leaders in each location, they will bond together as a cohesive group, and feed off each other's talents and experience. Many of them will become friends, not just business associates. And *as equity partners, they will each have a vested interest in the success of their operation, which will translate into success for the entire organization.* Bright, talented people like to associate with others of the same ilk. It's the old "birds of a feather flock together" syndrome. If you get it right, you will have a truly dynamic company. Garth Richards, one of the people joining our new moving consortium, is really excited about the new opportunity. He told me one of the reasons he agreed to be part of the group was because he really liked the people involved.

Never underrate the value of friendship among your employees and partners. There is a very real and tangible benefit for the company in these relationships. Most people don't like to leave their friends, so if your employees and partners become friends with each other, they are less likely to leave the company. It then stands to reason that when people stay at a company, their level of expertise increases as they mature in the business. This enhancement of their operating skills has a direct and positive impact on how smoothly things run, and on how profitable the company becomes. Similarly, people who have an equity stake in their operation are also less likely to depart. In my transportation company days, I took a lot of pride in the fact we had almost no turnover among our senior staff over a 20-year period. We are doing the same thing with our new venture, Premiere Executive Van Lines. The core group is made up of many of the people who were part of my former moving company. We have a bond of history, mutual respect, and a deep abiding friendship. I am confident these factors will contribute to our future success.

The corporate culture I have always strived for means that your operator/partners should be:

- bright and intelligent
- great in dealing with people
- talented in their field
- good problem solvers
- hard-working
- creative
- positive and enthusiastic
- energetic
- honest
- ethical
- good communicators
- fun-loving

Getting the right people in to key positions at each location will increase your chances for success. Good people produce good results.

Now that you have a taste for expansion, let's move on to real-life examples of my principles in action. When I left the moving business in 1999, I didn't have any specific plans to start another company. Over the years I had invested in a variety of other businesses, including Swiss Chalet restaurants and a chain of nursing homes. In those instances, I was simply a financial investor, not an operating partner. Most of my working years had been devoted to the moving business.

My entry into the world of temporary accommodations came about almost by accident, although the seeds of the idea had always been in the back of my mind. As a lifelong investor in real estate, I am always on the lookout for great properties. And as someone who spent most of my working life in the moving business, particularly the corporate employee relocation sector, I came to know a number of people in the extended-stay accommodation business. One is Tom Vincent, of Bridgestreet (the second largest of this type of firm in North America, with 9,000 units). I first met Tom 20 years ago when he owned his own company in Toronto, Executive Travel Apartments. He later sold it to the American giant Bridgestreet for millions, then went to work for them in Washington, D.C. Recently, he bought his company back and has returned to Canada.

We kept in touch over the years. I was very intrigued with his business since it revolved around real estate investment and it had some natural synergies with the moving industry. I remember talking to Tom about this back in 1991, telling him I really liked his business and actually declaring, "One day, I will be in it." We laughed about it. Little did we know it was only a matter of time before this actually happened.

For those of you who aren't familiar with the extended-stay accommodation business, I'll explain it briefly. It is an alternative to hotel accommodation. Clients include people who are relocating to a new city or who are sent on a temporary assignment. Others may be business travellers, short-term visitors, or vacationers. Some customers have had fires or floods in their own home or are temporarily displaced for other reasons.

Usually, the properties are furnished condominiums, apartments, and townhouses; in rare cases, they can be single family homes. Square footage can range from a minimum of 400 square feet to 2,000 square feet. The properties can be in large or small buildings or complexes. Corporations who relocate personnel (either on a permanent or temporary basis) are the main clientele. There are a number of reasons why they prefer this type of accommodation over that of conventional hotels, such as:

- lower daily cost — 30% to 40% less than hotels
- more comfortable accommodations
- all the amenities you have in your own home
  (full kitchens, laundry facilities, etc.)
- full range of services available at no or little extra cost
- no taxes charged on stays of 30 days or more
- no charge for local telephone calls

People being relocated often find it rather stressful to have to live in a hotel for any extended period. Hotel accommodations arranged by employers usually consist of a standard hotel room, so there's not a lot of space. Meals have to be eaten out at restaurants, and laundry has to be sent out, which adds to the cost of the stay and can be inconvenient.

My entry into this business began when I purchased a couple of condominiums in Halifax. It was my intention to dabble in the extended-stay accommodation business, but just as a sideline. I didn't plan to start another full-fledged business. After I furnished my two condominiums, I put an ad in the *Halifax Chronicle*. Almost immediately I was able to find two people who worked in the oil and gas industry who needed accommodations for a year and six months, respectively.

Besides the insights into the business that I gained from my friendship with Tom Vincent, I met another fellow in the business by the name of Dave Morton. I decided I would ask him some questions about the industry. Since I never went to business school, I make it a practice to learn from others who have been successful or have specific knowledge that I can use. Interestingly, Dave started out in a similar way to me, with a single condominium. Today, he and his wife, Doriana, own approximately 100 units. Dave was very helpful and very forthcoming with information and tips about his business, and I learned a great deal from him. I also found it refreshing that a competitor was willing to share information. I liked the sounds of the business, so I decided to try it on a very small scale. It worked so well, I continued to buy condominiums. By the time I had ten, I began to panic, because I didn't realize how much work was involved.

As the sole operator, my time was taken up dealing with decorators, buying furniture, arranging for cleaning, maintenance, and other services, plus handling all of the administrative details. I just didn't have time for it. I needed someone to run the business on a daily basis, so I called my friend Suzanne Bachur to see if she knew anyone suitable for the job. Suzanne and I have known each other for 27 years dating back to the time when she was the receptionist at my moving company's Toronto office. We remained close friends after she left AMJ Campbell and I even became an investor in the Swiss Chalet restaurants that she and her husband, Ron, own and operate in Nova Scotia. Suzanne was someone I respected and trusted, so I knew that anyone she recommended would be a good hire.

Much to my surprise, Suzanne told me she was ready for a break from the restaurant business, and would be interested in taking on the challenge herself. Her husband was agreeable to the idea. This was great news, because Suzanne was ideal for the job. She had all the necessary financial, administrative, and interpersonal skills needed for the new venture. With Suzanne running the day-to-day operations, I could devote my energies to expanding the business. So I immediately offered her the job and made her a 15% equity partner.

For those of you who are new to this concept, it meant that every time we purchased a property, Suzanne would have to put up 15% of the down payment and I would put up 85%. For example, if the property cost $200,000 then the down payment was 25% or $50,000. Suzanne's 15% share would cost her $7,500. The mortgage on the properties was carried by the cash flow generated by the operating company. By the end of the first year, we had 27 units, and we kept on buying. At the end of the first year, my accountant, Terry Carter, told me he hadn't wanted to say anything, but he was starting to think I had "lost it." He told me a story about a local doctor who purchased too much real estate and ended up going bankrupt. I told him, "Don't worry about it. Most of the properties I'm buying in the Halifax area are costing me less than $85,000, which is a real bargain in comparison to the cost of real estate in other cities. I'll buy 50 more, if I can get them at these prices."

By the end of the second year, Suzanne had put $164,000 into the company when she told me, "Tim, Ron and I are maxed out. We don't have any more money to invest right now." So, I brought in a couple of other investment partners, Jeff Somerville and Mark MacMillan. Before we knew it, we had over 100 properties in Halifax. We owned 40 of them and had taken over leases on the balance. That's when we decided to look at expanding into other centres. Premiere took responsibility for operating the company, which included decorating, cleaning, and maintaining the units, finding the customers, and handling the marketing and administrative functions. As the company grew, it needed more management expertise. In September 2002, Jeff Somerville, who was a former senior vice-president with TD Bank, decided to join Premiere as president. He invested $450,000 of his own money because he knew that real estate is always a good investment and he felt the company had a bright future. For a man who had always worked in a large corporate structure, Jeff found himself in a very different environment where he wore many hats. Eventually, Jeff left to pursue other interests but had contributed enormously to Premiere's growth during his tenure with the company.

By 2002, the company was valued at $5 million. We had been growing at a good pace, but I realized that in order to expand further we would need to bring in an investor with extensive resources. It was at this point that Dr. Jim Spatz and his partner Don Clow of Southwest Properties became a major partner in Premiere. Southwest is a well-known and highly respected company in the Maritimes. It is the largest owner of residential properties in Atlantic Canada and possesses approximately 40 apartment buildings and numerous shopping malls. Jim and Don viewed Premiere as an excellent investment — and today, Premiere Executive Suites is worth about $8 million and growing. To give you some idea of Premiere's expansion over the past five years or so, here are a few facts. It goes to show how quickly a company can grow if you have the right people and partners in place.

- Number of Branches   10
- Number of Units   500
- Dollars of Annual Revenue $12 Million
- Value of Real Estate $30 Million
- Number of Employees   100

Much of Premiere's success can be attributed to the fact that I did my utmost to recreate the business model and culture that had made my former multi-branch moving company so famous. You should never discount the importance of having a dynamic culture within your company. It really is what makes you stand out from your competition. I always advise other business owners to give this important area the attention it deserves. It is particularly critical that the corporate culture be weaved through the entire company, including all branches or sub-locations.

Getting outstanding people involved was the place to start. *I wanted all our operating partners, sales personnel, and employees to be exceptional individuals who would bring their own unique talents to the business.* Once again, I have been blessed and fortunate to find exactly the right people for this venture. I wanted hard-working, enthusiastic, intelligent, fun-loving people to help me grow the business. And, as I did with AMJ Campbell Van Lines, I reached out to people I knew and admired, or in a few cases to special individuals who were referred to me by people whom I trusted. Choosing the right employees and partners is a critical component in business today.

One example of an outstanding hire was Christine Bishop, who joined our Halifax office. From the moment I met her, I knew she would be a real asset to our company. Christine had a tremendous amount of experience in the hotel and accommodation business. She had worked with major companies in Scotland and Australia, and had been extremely successful throughout her career. She approached us shortly after she arrived in Halifax and we immediately offered her a job. Frankly, we were honoured that she would choose us, since we knew she could have had her pick of any employer. We were confident that she would be a wonderful addition to our group and she certainly didn't let us down. Her annual sales exceed $3 million, making her one of the top producers in our industry.

I'd also like to give you a sense of what a few of our operating partners have accomplished in a relatively short period. You've already been introduced to Suzanne Bachur in Halifax. She is the glue that holds the East Coast operations together. She is also a great help to each new franchisee who comes on board. My former executive assistant Kim Boydell and her partner Lois Roque (a former Bridgestreet employee) are turning in very impressive results in the west end of Toronto, with 80 properties (of which 40 are outsourced), $2 million in sales, and $150,000 in profit in just one year. Together, the two dynamic women own 45% of their branch. Claudine Savoie (former director of sales at the renowned Hotel Beauséjour in Moncton) is also doing an incredible job in our Moncton location. Here, we built our own 23-unit complex, at a cost of $3.5 million, to add to the few properties we already had in that city.

Another pair of women whom I am extremely proud of is the previously mentioned Tatiana Kredl, and her partner Judy Sandor, who own 47.5% and 5%

respectively of our Montreal operation. Tatiana is a natural entrepreneur. She understands the importance of promoting her business and knows the value of good public relations. Rather than spend a lot of money on advertising, Tatiana looks for creative ways to get the company in the news. Once, she called up the *Montreal Gazette* and asked to speak to a staff writer who specializes in writing about women entrepreneurs. She told the journalist about her success as a female entrepreneur at Premiere Executive Suites. The writer was intrigued and did a full interview and arranged for a photograph. The result was a two-page story in a major city newspaper. Within a few days of the article appearing, Tatiana was receiving more calls than usual inquiring about doing business with Premiere. The impact from this kind of positive press is far more valuable than paid advertising. People believe editorial, whereas they are sceptical of advertising.

In addition to articles in the press, Tatiana has done a lot of networking with the local Chamber of Commerce and enters into various competitions that are open to local businesses. In late 2004 I received a letter from Peter Yeoman, Mayor of Dorval, congratulating Premiere on being the "Heritage Award Winner of the 2004 Montreal Architectural Heritage Campaign." This honour was in addition to the Tourism and Hospitality Award we received from the Montreal Chamber of Commerce.

All of the Premiere locations have learned the value of public recognition and each of my partners in this wonderful company takes every opportunity to promote it in a variety of ways. More proof of this came in February 2005 when our Halifax location was honoured with the "Small Business of the Year Gold Award, Atlantic Canada."

Out west, our operating partner is none other than former Olympian, Order of Canada recipient, and holder of two honourary doctorate degrees, Diane Jones-Konihowski, and her husband John, a famous football star with the Edmonton Eskimos, who won five Grey Cups during his stellar career. Talk about name recognition! At the other end of the country, in Newfoundland, we have another very well-known partner, Bill Mahoney, who is one of the most respected businessmen in that province. Bill came to us via a recommendation from senior people at the Royal Bank. The day-to-day operations in St. John's are handled by Barb Williams, who is a real asset to Bill's organization. She is one of the most intelligent and fun-loving individuals I've ever met, so she fits right in with our corporate culture.

As an entrepreneur, it is possible to start small (as I did with those two condominiums) and then grow your business into a multi-location operation in a relatively short period of time. You don't always require extensive marketing studies, but you must have the right operators/partners and, of course, you need a great product or service. I think you can tell how proud I am of all of the people who have joined Premiere Executive Suites over the past five years.

I'm sometimes asked why we are doing so well with Premiere, when other companies in the same industry have experienced some reversals of fortunes. I think there are a few reasons. One is the quality and uniqueness of our product. At Premiere Executive Suites, we call our business "Your Home Away from Home," which really tells the whole story. We may be a small player, but we are rapidly gaining a reputation for our distinctive properties, such as waterfront buildings, historic houses, and inns — in other words, places that radiate character and individuality. These are our specialty, and they give us an edge in an otherwise crowded market. In addition, Premiere employs the services of a number of talented interior designers to make each unit warm, inviting, unique, and creatively decorated. We don't believe in having all of our units look the same, as is the case with some of our competitors. Instead, we use designers like Marie Harvey and Meredith Rochman to work with us to decorate our units. Each of our decorators has her own sense of style, a flare for colour, fabrics, and those extra special touches that turn each unit into a warm, inviting home away from home.

We have been successful in expanding this business, as I did previously with AMJ Campbell and fully intend to do in the future with my new endeavour, Premiere Van Lines. Each business has grown or will grow using my time-tested business practices that have worked for me and can work for you:

- Maintaining a strong financial position
- Seizing opportunities when the time is right
- Bringing in the right partners
- Creating a corporate culture that is conducive to entrepreneurial pursuits
- Gaining public recognition for the company
- Differentiating the product from the competition

KEY LESSONS LEARNED

- Expansion on a national basis allows you to maximize your company's potential in other markets
- Never expand until you have a solid financial foundation
- Market analysis doesn't have to be complex
- "Analysis paralysis" can lead to missed opportunities
- The right operator for a new location is essential
- Seek out information from people already in the business
- Use a creative formula to bring in equity partners
- Put a unique spin on your operation to differentiate it from the competition

CHAPTER SIX

WAR STORIES

"If you find a path with no obstacles, it probably doesn't lead anywhere."
— *Frank A. Clark*

In chapter 4, I provided you with an overview of my former moving company and highlighted some of its major achievements. By the time I semi-retired in 1999 to assume the role of advisory chairman, the company had attained legendary status throughout the moving and relocation related industries. We had a corporate culture envied by all our peers, our salespeople were renowned, and our exploits made front-page news on a regular basis. But all of this success did not come without some major battles.

I have always been prepared to do whatever was needed to ensure my company's survival. On occasion, this meant bending the rules. In this chapter I'd like to recount a few of my more famous war stories so you fully understand the lengths you should be prepared to go to in order to protect your business.

Every company will encounter obstacles at various points in their history. As the leader of your company,

you are the one who must decide how far you are prepared to go to overcome them. In my opinion, great
leaders are the ones who are prepared to go to battle for
the sake of their companies' well-being. It's been my
experience that the larger the organization, the larger
the battles that must be fought. People have often said
I thrive on challenges and actually enjoy battles. I'll
admit this is an accurate assessment. In a strange way, I
find these situations to be quite invigorating. Perhaps
I feel this way because a good battle gives me the
opportunity to do one of the things that I do best —
find solutions to what seem like unsolvable problems.
Like many entrepreneurs, I get a little bored when
things are going too smoothly.

While I am always up for a challenge, I most definitely go into battle mode when I feel there is an
injustice being done or people are acting in an unprofessional manner. When this happens, I don't shy away
from conflict. Instead, I hit the issue head on. At the
outset, I try to resolve the problem with the specific individual involved. If this approach is not successful, then I
am not averse to going over their head to the highest
level until I find someone to give us a fair hearing.

For example, back in 1988, Imperial Oil's corporate
moving contract went to tender. There were 250 moves
per year at stake so this was a rather large contract. The
problem for my company was that Imperial decided to
restrict the bidding to the four major van lines rather
than allow the moving companies who actually
perform the physical services to bid. I could understand
their rationale at not wanting to deal with small
moving companies, but my firm was unique. We were
the only coast-to-coast multi-branch mover in the

country and as such we had the infrastructure and resources to service this client's requirements. I also knew that we could be more price competitive if the contract was awarded directly to us than if it came through our van line. I asked that we be allowed to bid on the contract but my request was declined. I'm sure they expected us to accept their decision and go away quietly, but that isn't the end of the story.

Around the same time, I appeared on the CBC business show Venture. During the filming for the show, CBC's crew taped me having a conversation with a representative from Imperial Oil wherein I was questioning their decision not to let us bid on their business. When the show aired to approximately two million viewers, CBC included a picture of Imperial Oil's head office as a backdrop to the story. I learned through a friend, Mike Hollihan (whose brother had a senior position at the oil company), that Imperial was thinking of suing my company for the remarks I had made during the television interview. In the end, Imperial Oil never took action against us. In fact, we eventually started doing business with them, first through our commercial office moving division. Eventually we were also awarded their employee relocation business.

Sometimes you have to have the courage of your convictions and be prepared to fight for what you think is right. Many people thought I was crazy to publicly criticize a major corporation on national television. They told me there would be dire consequences to my actions. However, I felt strongly that we were being treated unfairly and I was prepared to take my chances.

My experience with Imperial Oil was not the only time I have challenged major corporations. Over the years, I have gone to many CEOs and senior managers of various organizations to complain about the unprofessional treatment received at the hands of one or more of their employees. When business is at stake, I will go to any lengths to be given a fair hearing. The secret to this approach is to do it in a totally professional manner. At all times, you must be diplomatic and sincere. It doesn't hurt to exhibit a touch of humility. Even if you don't get what you want the first time around, at least you have set the stage for a future opportunity. Being the head of a company means you have to be tenacious and determined to fight for business. Sitting back and waiting for the telephone to ring won't pay the bills.

One of my primary functions has always been to sell and market the company's services. As the president of the company, I find it is relatively easy to arrange meetings with potential clients. Titles do make a difference, which is one reason I have always advocated impressive titles for our sales personnel. Instead of just putting "Sales Consultant" on a card, I recommend you have your salespeople use the term "Executive Consultant" or "Client Relationship Consultant" or something similar. The goal is to be a little bit different.

Sometimes, though, individuals seem determined not to give you or your salespeople an opportunity to discuss how your product or service could benefit them. As we all know, sales are the lifeblood of any organization. Without sales, your company won't survive. This means you can't be fainthearted in going after new business. In my businesses, there are a finite number of available customers for our services. This is particularly true on the corporate employee relocation side of moving. In Canada, there is only a relatively small percentage of companies who transfer more than 100 employees each year. Large contracts are rare. Therefore, when these opportunities arise, I understand how crucial it is to try to secure a portion of this business.

I also understand and respect a company's right to remain with an existing supplier. Obviously, I wouldn't want my clients turning their business over to a competitor. At the same time, I believe it's only good business for a corporate purchaser to know who else is out there who could service their business, should a change be required at some future date. This is why I don't appreciate people who refuse to at least have a brief meeting. Even companies who have long-standing relationships with a specific supplier should be interested in knowing what the competition has to offer. If nothing else, it gives them a basis for comparison and may help keep their existing supplier on their toes.

I make sure that I am very professional in my approach and therefore I get quite irked when I encounter rude people. I don't believe rudeness is ever acceptable. Buyers who don't want to see salespeople should at least be respectful and professional when they decline an invitation to meet. If the individual is particularly out-of-line or very unprofessional then I am not averse to complaining about the treatment to someone at a higher level in the company.

On the other side of the coin, I try to make time to meet with people who are attempting to sell something to me, providing they act in a professional manner. I'd like to tell you about one such situation that started out well but ended badly due to unprofessionalism on the part of a salesperson. This young man worked for

Manulife Insurance. He called to arrange an appointment and because I was travelling extensively at the time, he talked to my executive assistant, Kim Boydell. She explained that I was currently unavailable but promised him that I would meet with him as soon as my schedule allowed. In good salesman fashion, this fellow followed up on a regular basis and eventually the appointment was made.

When I met with him, I was very impressed. He was personable, knowledgeable about his products, and seemed very professional. Unfortunately for him, as good as his sales pitch was, I wasn't really in the market for any of the products he was selling. However, I told him we might be interested in hiring him, if he decided on a career change. I told him to think about my offer and get back to me.

By the time he started to call back, I was on the road again and he was back to dealing with my assistant. This time, his true colours came to the forefront. He was arrogant and rude with Kim when she tried to explain that I was out of town and might not be able to call him back immediately. When I heard about this, I called him and told him that we could never hire a person who would treat an assistant the way he had treated Kim. In my world, every person you deal with, regardless of position or rank, deserves respect and courtesy. There's no room in any of my businesses for a person who saves their professional demeanour for senior management only.

My willingness to do battle also extends to tackling existing customers who are abusing our employees. I recall a former client who was using the most abusive language imaginable with one of our claims adjusters,

Ret Brown. This employee was renowned for her efficiency and her sensitivity in dealing with customers, so I knew she did nothing to provoke this man. In fact, Ret wasn't the person who brought this situation to my attention. One of her colleagues witnessed how upset she became after a telephone encounter with this man and felt I should know about it.

I instructed Ret to transfer the call to me the next time this person telephoned, which she did. I spoke to the man and apologized for the mistake that we had made, which resulted in his having to file a claim. I assured him that the problem would be rectified. I then brought up what I really wanted to discuss. I told him that our company always treats our customers with dignity and respect and that we treat our employees in the same manner. I told him that I simply couldn't tolerate abusive behaviour directed towards a staff member who is only trying to help him. I figured I had made my point and I concluded by telling him to call me directly should he have any other concerns about our service. I don't know if it was my position in the company or the fact that I was another man, but he seemed to understand what I was saying. I thought the matter was resolved.

Then, about two weeks later, he called Ret and again started using abusive and foul language. She transferred the call to me. I came on the line and told him that I thought we already had an understanding about this type of behaviour on his part. Then he started in on me in a very aggressive manner. I'd had enough and decided to give him a taste of his own medicine, although profanity is not part of my normal lexicon. I just figured I had to fight fire with fire. The next day I received a letter from his solicitor accusing me of abusing his client. He quoted what I had said to this man. I called the lawyer and told him I had no idea what he was talking about. Everyone who knows me knows this would be totally out of character. I suggested his client should be more careful in his own use of language when talking to people. That was the last we heard from this man or his lawyer. I'm sure that he bad-mouthed our company to every person he came in contact with, but as much as I hate to lose business, I won't allow my employees to be intimidated or abused by anyone. The moral of the story is that sometimes you have to stand up to a customer when they are in the wrong. As entrepreneurs, we like to live by the adage "The customer is always right," but if it means an employee has to be abused in the process then all bets are off.

The next battle I'd like to talk about was with a somewhat more formidable foe — the Teamsters Union — but their clout didn't stop me from taking them on. When I purchased MJ Campbell in 1977, I inherited a union shop. At the time, I was still naïve so I didn't fully understand the implications. About a month after the purchase, I received two grievance complaints from our Barrie office. Two of our employees were complaining about something. I don't recall the exact nature of the complaints, but they seemed to be petty issues. Since I had never dealt with unions before, I didn't really know what to expect. Still, no one was going to tell me how to run my company. I had a good track record with employees as long as they had a good attitude, and I did my best to create an excellent working environment. Rather than approach me directly with their issues, the two employees insisted on dealing with their union representative. I had no choice but to agree to a meeting.

I was prepared to stand my ground and be tough with them. The men who arrived at my office were the stereotypical image of Teamsters — big burly guys each weighing 250 to 300 pounds. In spite of their appearance, I refused to be intimidated. I told them my views and said if they persisted in trying to harass me, I would sell the business or just shut it down. From that point on I was determined to get the union out of my business. One day, I insisted that one of the two men who had filed the grievance accompany me on two long-distance jobs to pack, load, and deliver a shipment to Belleville and St. Catharines. I knew this was outside of his regular job description so I was expecting trouble. He was older than I was, and up to this point I had found him quite ornery and uncommunicative. Surprisingly, once we spent time working and travelling together, we began to establish a good relationship.

Eventually, the union backed off and agreed that as long as we signed an annual union contract to take care of just two named employees they would leave us alone. Twenty years later both men retired. Shortly thereafter, we got a call from a union official who wanted to come in to talk. I invited him to come by for coffee and a chat. Again, the stereotype of a Teamster boss arrived. He was even bigger than his comrades from years past and had the largest hands I've ever seen, but I was determined to end this thing once and for all. By then, we had over 400 full- and part-time personnel so a union contract was the last thing I wanted. I made it quite clear that there would be no more annual contracts. I knew we had a good working relationship with our drivers. In fact, we had changed the compensation plan over to a shared revenue arrangement instead of hourly pay so a union deal wouldn't be that attractive to them. I can only assume our employees must have told the union organizer they weren't interested in forming a union, because that visit was the last I ever saw of anyone from the Teamsters Union.

In business, you occasionally find yourself in conflict with people or organizations with whom you are associated. This has happened to me a few times over the years, especially in the moving business. My company became an agent for Atlas Van Lines in 1984, and for the most part, it was a wonderful association. However, business is business. There have been times when I have had to go head-to-head with Atlas's president, Doug Auld, over issues that affected my company. Doug and I are good personal friends outside of the business arena, but that never meant we couldn't disagree.

I recall one major issue that involved Nortel, which at the time was a strong, vibrant company. The firm was actively transferring nearly 1,000 employees per year across North America, and a tender was issued. Our company and a large Atlas Van Lines agent in the United States were both asked to bid. It was agreed we would submit a single bid, and that intra-Canada and southbound moves to the U.S. would go to our company, and the intra-U.S.A. and northbound moves to Canada would go to the American agent. We won the contract. Everything was fine until Nortel decided to move their relocation department's responsibilities to Nashville, Tennessee. The U.S. agent immediately jumped on this, and convinced the giant firm that all moves should go through *their* office. With this much business at stake, I couldn't just stand back, so I insisted on having a conference call with all the senior executives of both the Canadian and American van line offices, as well as that of the U.S. agent who was involved. It was not a pleasant call. A few of the players indicated they had never really agreed to the terms. For one of the few times in my career, I just lost it during this call. I'm not proud of the way I spoke to these people, but frankly, the stakes were too high to try to play nice. Subsequently, we worked things out, and enjoyed a good working relationship with each other throughout the duration of the contract.

One of the points I'm trying to make with this last story is that while you might disagree with business associates, it should be done *without* it becoming personal. Something I have always admired about Doug Auld was that we could do battle, and vehemently disagree, and yet we were able to separate those tense occasions from our personal relationship and friendship. To me, that is the mark of a real gentleman.

Being in business means dealing with problems and difficult situations. Not every problem is a major battle, but it sometimes seems that way. The worst thing you can do in this regard is procrastinate. I've always believed that for every problem or challenge, there is a solution. You can't solve problems if you are afraid to make decisions. Some of those decisions will be right and a few will be wrong. *Just make a decision.* Your time is valuable. If you are going to succeed in business, you won't have the luxury of taking forever to make a decision — otherwise, nothing will ever get accomplished.

As an entrepreneur, I make decisions daily, and I have made more than my fair share of mistakes. When

I bought six condominiums in Moncton for Premiere Executive Suites, it was the first time I had bought condos in that province and I was unfamiliar with their property tax regulations. I never imagined the regulations would be any different from Nova Scotia, Ontario, or Alberta where I had made similar purchases. But in New Brunswick and Prince Edward Island, any condominiums that are not your personal residence are taxed at a rate almost double that of what one would expect. This meant that a small 1,050-square-foot unit is taxed at $5,000 per year, almost the same as what I pay for a 3,200-square-foot condo in the luxury Palace Pier complex in Toronto! I was flabbergasted when I learned about this rule. To me, it is a real deterrent to real estate investment. And because the regulation doesn't exist in other provinces, I got blindsided. It was my own fault because I didn't do my homework. It didn't take long before I decided to put the six condos up for sale.

Yet, I didn't let this little fiasco sour me on the idea of investing in Moncton. Due to a favourable tax ruling, we were able to approach our Moncton business from another angle. We decided to invest over $3.5 million in our *own* multi-level building, which contains 23 units. It was completed in November 2004, and the best part is the units will be taxed at approximately $2,200 per year.

Every business person is faced with a variety of problems. ***Problems don't go away on their own.*** Many people have a tendency to put off dealing with serious problems. I've learned it is crucial to put closure to problems as quickly as you can. They will only magnify and get worse if you procrastinate. Furthermore, a delay in dealing with issues shows a weakness in your ability to operate effectively and efficiently.

When staff members or partners approach me with a problem, they often preface their remarks by asking, "Do you want the good news or the bad news first?" I always respond by telling them to give me the bad news, because I'd rather tackle the problem immediately. Treat problems as opportunities. If you don't handle them, then you will likely find that they will fester and become more serious.

If a customer has a problem or a complaint, procrastination will only serve to make them angrier and more determined to get something from you. On the other hand, a problem that is taken care of quickly can lead to increased goodwill and future business from this same customer or people they may refer to your company. Most people understand that sometimes mistakes are made. When this happens, you have an opportunity to make it right, providing you act in a timely manner. If a customer feels they had to fight to get their problem resolved, they will see it as a negative situation. However, if they bring a problem to your attention and you make a quick and mutually acceptable decision, then you gain some goodwill for your efforts. Your company is seen in a positive light, in spite of the original problem.

I've always made it a practice to *be extremely accessible, and to personally handle serious problems.* This is something I would recommend to all entrepreneurs. Don't leave it to lower-level staff or third parties to handle these types of situations for you. As the owner of the company, you are in a much better position to negotiate a resolution to a problem, and if you demonstrate compassion and genuine regret, you can often do it in such a way as to minimize the damage and/or costs to your company.

As you can appreciate, the moving industry is one in which there is always the potential for serious customer issues. I recall one unusual situation that required all of my customer service skills. Our company was storing some household possessions that were valued at over $1 million. The owners of the goods were two women from Iran. Their belongings remained in storage for a long period, and the account often fell into arrears for a month or two. Then a cheque would arrive to bring the account up to date. At one point, however, the account was in arrears by several months. Normally, practice would dictate that the person in charge of storage accounts would make every effort to collect the outstanding money. If the situation cannot be rectified, eventually the goods would go to auction. Before it reaches that stage, there are a series of legal steps dictated by the Warehouseman's Lien Act. Unfortunately, in this situation the storage accounts clerk, who was relatively new, approached the branch manager about her inability to collect the money. The manager authorized her to send the goods to auction. They made a critical error by not following the proper legal steps. The goods went to auction without the owners' knowledge.

A month or two after the auction, the owners contacted us to bring their account up to date. These two women were devastated when they learned what had transpired. At first, they both refused to believe their furniture, art, and family artifacts were all gone. I was asked to intervene, and after notifying our insurance company about a potentially large claim, I invited the two women to the office to meet with me, and discuss the matter. Many company owners would have just turned the matter over to the lawyers and the insurance company, but I felt a personal responsibility to the customers for our firm's error. It was a very emotional meeting.

The women refused to shake my hand when I greeted them, which was something I had never encountered in the past. However, by the end of that first meeting, some three hours later, they did shake my hand before departing. I felt this was progress. During our lengthy meeting, I learned that the two women were members of the Iranian Royal Family and that many of the items contained in the storage lot were priceless antiques and irreplaceable. I started having nightmares about how much money this claim would cost, and what it would do to our insurance premiums (assuming that our insurance company would even agree to pay for the loss, considering that proper procedures had not been followed).

After numerous meetings, I established a warm relationship with the customers, and I felt the claim could be handled in a professional manner. To my total amazement, the customers *never* filed a claim. To this day, I will never understand why. So, while this is far from normal, it does prove that **sometimes you can diffuse a bad situation by becoming personally involved.**

By contrast, here's an example of handling things the *wrong* way. In 2004, I heard about a situation involving two top-performing salespeople who had resigned from my former moving company. When they left, management refused to pay their outstanding commissions. The employees had to threaten to sue their former employer. One of the people involved sued for $10,000 in outstanding commissions. The company offered $5,000 and told him that if he didn't accept, it would counter-sue him for $200,000 for lost business. He refused the offer and the counter-suit was launched. The irony of the situation was that, while the company was suing this person, it was trying to re-hire him. The case dragged on for more than six months. By that time word about the lawsuit had leaked out to the industry, which hurt the company's reputation. This was a classic case of doing things the wrong way.

I would also like to pass on a piece of advice about the way you handle your daily workload. While this might be viewed more as a time management topic, I think there is some correlation to one's ability to deal with problems. I've known other executives who were so disorganized, they just didn't know where to start. With stacks of papers or files on their desk, they were often tempted to just ignore them all, thus delaying decisions even further. One senior person in the moving industry was known to tell subordinates he piled files up on his credenza, and if no one came to ask about them for several months, he'd just send them back to the file room.

I have found that the only way I can keep on top of all I have to do, which includes making hundreds of decisions each week, is to stay organized. Don't be one of those people who shuffle papers around endlessly on your desk, or create large, unorganized piles of paper. Experts will tell you *clutter is something you want to avoid at all costs; it is draining from both a mental and physical perspective.* You will expend more time and energy trying to find things than you would if you had just dealt with things the first time they passed through your hands. My mantra is: Do . . . Delegate . . . Dispose . . . or File. In his bestselling book, *What They Don't Teach You at Harvard Business School*, author Mark McCormack gives this advice: "Organize for the next day at the end of the previous day. This is what gives me peace of mind at night and the feeling that I am on top of things."

KEY LESSONS LEARNED

- Be prepared to fight for your company
- Don't be intimidated by others
- Stand up for your employees even if you lose business as a result
- Attack the issue, not the individual — never make it personal
- Learn to trust your instincts
- Make decisions — don't procrastinate, especially when fixing mistakes
- As company owner, handle serious problems personally
- Get organized

CHAPTER SEVEN

THE PARTNERS
PLAYBOOK

*"What matters is working with people you trust and respect, knowing that
if times turn bad these people would hold together."*
— Sir Richard Branson

I would *not* be where I am today if it were not for the
many business partners I have had over the years.
Almost without exception, these experiences have been
positive ones. Even where the situation was not ideal,
the partnership served an important purpose, and my
real-world business education was advanced.

While I welcome and appreciate partners who are
just interested in making a financial investment, my real
joy comes from finding those exceptional people who
will make outstanding operating partners in my various
businesses. I suppose these partners appeal to the mentor in me. I take the greatest amount of satisfaction in
seeing other people fulfill their potential and become
financially successful. Many of the greatest success
stories I can recount are about people that most would
not have expected to have what it takes to be a great
entrepreneur. I wish there was space to tell you about

all of them, but for purposes of illustration, I'll talk about three special individuals.

My one-time receptionist at my moving firm, Suzanne Bachur, is a shining example of someone with hidden talents. Her first foray into entrepreneurship began when she and her husband purchased a Swiss Chalet franchise in Halifax. I went in with them as an investment partner. Suzanne's husband, Ron, had been a field consultant for the McDonald's Corporation, so he had a good base of knowledge for this type of business. Suzanne had little direct experience in running a restaurant, but she soon proved she had what it took to be a successful entrepreneur. Today, Suzanne and Ron own three Swiss Chalet restaurants. They have become millionaires through hard work and shrewd investment. And as I've already mentioned, Suzanne decided to take a break from the restaurant business and joined me as a managing partner at Premiere Executive Suites. The skills and talent she honed at Swiss Chalet are now being used to help us grow our hospitality business.

Another friend, Mike Savoy, had worked as a truck driver in my first moving company, TC Moore Transport, in the 1970s. Later, he joined me at AMJ Campbell, first as a driver, then as operations manager. When the opportunity arose to purchase a franchise, Mike jumped at the chance. A few years later, he relocated to the East Coast, and eventually became my partner in our Halifax and Montreal moving company franchises, a self-storage business, and in a number of commercial properties. Today, Mike is a well-established millionaire.

My brother Terry left a secure job as a sales manager for Phillips Electronics to join me as an entrepreneur in the moving business. He made a huge success out of his

Calgary-based company, which he took from zero to $14 million in a decade. Then he became a partner in a Premiere Executive Suites franchise in Alberta, going from zero to $2 million in a few short years. Like me, Terry chose the right partners for each of his various business ventures. He understood how important it is to mentor aspiring entrepreneurs and to give them a chance to succeed in their own right. Today, he and his partners are devoting their time and talents to building another successful moving company in Calgary.

In the past, the majority of my partners were men; however, the pendulum has swung the other way with Premiere Executive Suites, where all but one of the operating partners are women. This was not by design or intention, but I must say that it is working out extraordinarily well. Women are naturally drawn to the nature of the business. They have a genuine desire to be of assistance to people, and to ensure that they are happy and comfortable. Women also tend to be more caring and nurturing than men. They are prepared to go beyond the call of duty to ensure our clients are pleased with the services rendered.

I thoroughly enjoy working with women because they generally have the ideal combination of creativity and practicality. At the risk of sounding sexist, I also find that women tend to be less ego-driven than men. Women can be strong and confident in their abilities, and yet they rarely develop the kind of arrogance that too often afflicts successful men. I recall someone telling me a story recently about a male executive who would dial into the company intercom and bellow, "Someone get me a coffee." It's doubtful any woman would ever consider doing such a rude thing.

Women are usually strong team players and excellent motivators. Consequently, they are often more successful than men, especially in smaller businesses. (Recent business surveys consistently show female entrepreneurs are less likely to take too much money out of a fledgling business.) Women also seem to know instinctively that playing the "I am the boss" card is not the ideal way to get your employees to work harder. Women usually lead by example. They are willing to pitch in with the most mundane tasks, and won't ask anyone to do anything they are unwilling to do themselves. Women entrepreneurs can be extraordinary role models for others who have similar career aspirations.

The only minor downside (if it really is one) that I've seen with women partners is their natural caution as it relates to taking risks. But, to be fair, this may be more of a positive attribute in certain circumstances. I am quite a risk taker, but I can afford the losses if things don't work out. Newly minted entrepreneurs probably need to err more on the side of caution, at least until they are fully established.

Partners can come from all walks of life. Over the years, I have had hundreds of partners. Choosing a business partner is a little bit like choosing a mate. Compatibility is paramount, since you will be spending a lot of time with each other. Personally, I have never advertised for a partner or sought one through an agency or consultant. As with regular employees, most of the people I have partnered with (either in a majority or minority arrangement) have been people I already knew, had worked with, or at least had contact with, in their natural working environment. Some were introduced to me through clients or employees.

The number one prerequisite in a partner is attitude. Here are some of the questions I would suggest you ask yourself when evaluating an individual to join you in a partnership arrangement:

- How do they get along with people?
- Are they respected by their peers?
- Are they hard workers?
- Will they fit in with the existing corporate culture?
- Do they stand out above the crowd of others in their field?
- Are they exceptional individuals in terms of past achievements, academic credentials, or personality?
- Are they good people/fun people?
- Are they happy and optimistic?
- Do they lead a balanced life?
- Are they aggressive in a constructive way?
- Do they thrive on challenges?
- Are they prepared to make sacrifices to achieve their goals and dreams?

With major partners, where you share equal or nearly equal responsibility for running the company, it is usually best that they have complementary skills with yours. This way, you can draw on each other's strengths. It's not always necessary to be close friends or have a personal relationship outside of business, but in my experience this helps make the partnership stronger. *A matching work ethic, similar goals, and a compatible business philosophy are ingredients for a successful partnership.* When one or more are missing, then the possibility for future problems becomes more likely.

Overall, I am very much in favour of partnerships.

You share the risk, the work, the rewards. But sometimes an arrangement with major or equal partners can be problematic, especially over the long run. My first experience with a majority partner could have soured me on the whole idea of partners, but it didn't. The arrangement wasn't exactly ideal, but it did teach me some valuable lessons.

I became co-owner of MJ Campbell Moving and Storage with my former accountant. This gave me an entry into a world to which I might not have otherwise been given access. I knew early on that my relationship with my partner would not survive for too long due to our very different business styles. However, I was prepared to make the best of it.

My first partner was a well-connected and shrewd businessman who was always on the lookout for new investments. When we went in together to buy the company, we were convinced it would be a smart investment. The prospect of being in partnership with someone who obviously had much more business experience than I did was the real draw for me. To be frank, I was still young and naïve enough to be flattered that he had wanted me to be his partner. We purchased the company for $200,000, which was a bargain.

At the time I went into this deal, I knew my partner had already been through several partnerships, which was not a good omen. Regardless, I needed him as much as he needed me, so I decided it might be a case of "the wrong partner but at the right time." Unfortunately, aside from our different approach to business, it quickly became apparent that I was the one doing most of the work, while my partner was enjoying a disproportionate amount of the rewards.

While it is true that he handled all the accounting and financial side of the business, it was left to me to do everything else, including learning how to function in a van line environment, which was fraught with countless rules and regulations. I was responsible for sales, operations, customer service, employee relations, opening new offices, hiring staff, and liaison with Van Line officials. It was an overwhelming amount of responsibility. My partner's responsibilities were more like a part-time job, so he was able to continue servicing other clients even though he drew the same salary as I did. In addition, he took full advantage of being a company owner and gave himself a number of costly perks. I began to resent the unfairness of the situation.

As time went on and the company grew, I began to realize we were getting over-extended and were poised for trouble unless we got things under control. A time came when we required a bulge in our line of credit, and the bank asked for $25,000 in personal guarantees. I immediately agreed. A few months later, while having lunch with an employee from the bank, I learned that my partner had never put up his own guarantee. To make matters worse, when I confronted him about it, he didn't think that what he did (or rather did not do) was anything important. It was one more example of our different approach to business. I felt it was only a matter of time before we would have to go our separate ways.

We soon decided it would make sense for one of us to buy the other out. After much negotiation, we agreed on a figure of $400,000. Suddenly, the partner who, up until then, had not had much interest in the business was very anxious to buy *me* out. I was puzzled. I had expected him to happily take his profits and move on to his next venture. Unbeknownst to me, my partner had recruited Dave McLean, a vice-president with North American Van Lines, to invest in the company and take my place in running it. Fortunately for me, my lawyer turned the tables on my partner at our final meeting, and because he was so sure he could take advantage of me, my partner foolishly responded to my lawyer's challenge. The happy result was that I ended up buying *him* out. I came out of this experience more competent and with a greater confidence in my abilities as an entrepreneur. I also knew I would never allow anyone to take advantage of me in the future.

Moving forward wasn't that easy, though, because of the financial mess left behind by my former partner. Since he was the financial expert, I had trusted his decisions. I didn't realize that he had put the company in serious jeopardy through his business practices. In 1981, our credit line was maxed out at $450,000 — at the worst possible time in our business cycle. We were in severe financial straits. Things were so bad that our bank told us to go elsewhere, but no other bank would accept us. My brother Ted, who worked with me, agreed to help. Together we borrowed $100,000 against our personal assets to help pay down our line of credit, and then spent the next year working long and hard to turn things around. During that time, we did not take one nickel out of the company. Within 12 months, we had paid down our line, and had $250,000 in the bank. Then we switched banks.

A couple of years later, I opened the door to a new partnership, with another chartered accountant. With the lessons learned from the first failed partnership still fresh in my mind, I entered this new arrangement as a more seasoned entrepreneur. By then I knew the importance of establishing a few ground rules in advance if I wanted to avoid problems in the future.

Here are some basic issues partners need to address before they enter into a partnership:

- How will decisions be made?
- Who has the ultimate authority, should agreement not be reached?
- Who will be the face of the company to the outside world?
- What mechanisms are in place to sever the relationship, if it becomes necessary to do so?

These are difficult issues, but they need to be addressed if your partnership is to work effectively. It is easier to deal with them up-front, rather than in the heat of the moment when a problem arises.

One person doesn't usually possess all of the skills needed to build a very large business. This is why partners should have complementary skills. Some entrepreneurs choose only to hire managers who have the skills that they themselves lack. Either way, it is important to have the right kind of expertise available; otherwise, crucial segments of the business may not get the attention they deserve.

If you go the partner route, the secret is to make sure each partner clearly understands the value of what the other partner brings to the table. As a rule, entrepreneurs tend to be more oriented towards the sales, marketing, and people-motivation side of the business. While I respect the knowledge and skill required to be in charge of a company's finances, I feel the sales and marketing role is the more crucial one. As that old saying goes, "Nothing happens until a sale is made." Chief financial officers might think otherwise.

I recall a deal I put together with the TD Bank that was worth $1.5 million to $2 million in incremental business. To get it, I had offered an extra 5% discount. I thought it was a brilliant move on my part. I was so excited about the coup that I couldn't wait to tell my partner. You can't imagine how disappointed I was when he had a negative reaction to my news. He fixated on the money given away in the form of an extra 5% discount while I was focused on the increase in business; obviously our mindsets were not the same.

In my opinion, partnerships where each party has a high level of expertise are win/win situations. As well, I have learned that all partnerships serve a purpose at a particular point in a company's history. I also know that partnerships don't necessarily last forever; circumstances change, people's priorities change, and human emotions often enter into the picture.

Over the past 25 years, I have had three major partners. Each partnership ended for specific reasons, but in each case, all three partners benefited financially from our relationship. Two of them netted over $1 million dollars in a relatively short period of time. Once a company is well established, partners may find they have reached a point where they want different things. One may want a greater challenge while the other may want fewer responsibilities and more personal time. It's easy to get out of synch with each other. Many factors affect the dynamics of a partnership, which is one reason why you must do your utmost to keep the lines of communication open. Problems can also occur when one partner begins to believe they are not receiving the recognition they deserve. I have to admit, I personally put some strain on my second major partnership when I decided to move to the East Coast, work from there, and commute back and forth to head office in Toronto. Looking back, I realize this arrangement was not fair to my partner.

Larry Papernick and I had become partners in 1983. I was president and CEO of the company, and he was executive vice-president and CFO. I held more shares than he did, but we considered ourselves to be relatively equal. I was responsible for the sales, marketing, and recruiting side of the business, while he handled all the administrative and financial functions. Each of us had our own particular areas of expertise, which made for a good partnership. The company was relatively large by then and needed the kind of structure and systems that were beyond my own capabilities. I felt my time was better spent developing new business and bringing in new people. I was happy to turn the other areas over to Larry. We were expanding into new centres on a regular basis, and our reputation as one of the most service-oriented companies in our industry made it possible for us to take business away from more established competitors. Times were good for both of us.

There were plenty of challenges to keep us busy, yet some fractures were starting to show in our relationship. The problems we eventually encountered were a result of a number of factors. Most of them were common to any rapidly expanding business being run by two strong-willed individuals. In our case, the problems were exacerbated by the fact that, while I was president of the company, I was away from the day-to-day operations for long periods of time. I had purchased a home in Chester, Nova Scotia, just south of Halifax, and by 1989 was spending more time there.

I recall being interviewed on CBC Radio by the late Peter Gzowski, wherein I expounded on the marvels of technology and the pleasures of working from a remote location. At the time, I felt I had the best of both worlds. Looking back on it now, however, I realize that it wasn't as effective as I had thought or hoped it would be. I lost some measure of control over the day-to-day affairs of the company by virtue of my absence. This arrangement gave others the opportunity to advance their own agendas. I realize now that our employees needed face time with the person in charge, and since I wasn't there, they went to my partner instead.

Some of his decisions were contrary to the ones I would have made. But in fairness to him, he was there, decisions had to be made, and Larry did what he thought best. I share this story as a cautionary tale. If, as an entrepreneur, you decide you want to pursue other interests or work a little less, then perhaps it makes sense to give up your title, and the control implicit in it, to the person you designate. You can't be in charge if you are not present. Management from a distance just isn't a workable solution for most businesses.

Since I was at the point of wanting more free time and my partner wanted more responsibility, I decided to resign. Larry became president of the company, but because I wanted to remain part of the company, I did not sell my shares. This kept me emotionally and fiscally tied to the company. In retrospect, it might have been better if I had made a clean break, instead of remaining in an altered partnership arrangement.

A combination of circumstances, which included a major recession and a lack of control over the company's finances, made it necessary for me to return to the company full time in 1991, to help turn things around. I was reinstated as president and CEO and my partner resumed his former role as executive vice-president and CFO. It was no secret that he wasn't happy with this turn of events. These changes were difficult partly because some of our managers and employees felt they had to take sides. It was not a particularly pleasant time around the company as we struggled to survive. We had to make some radical changes in the way the company operated — 25 employees were let go, managers took pay cuts, and everyone did their part.

By the time things were back on track, my relationship with my partner was not in good shape. Eventually, he decided to resign. I'm sorry to say that we parted on less than friendly terms. Fortunately, over time, Larry and I reconnected on a personal level, and are on friendly terms again.

A partnership doesn't break up without some warning. There are usually signs that all is not well. The trouble is, we don't always like to admit there are problems, so we carry on in the hopes that things will get better. It is far better to face up to things before they reach a crisis stage. Here are a few major signs to be on the alert for:

- Too many problems cropping up at one time
- Decisions being made without adequate (or any) discussion between partners
- Undermining of authority or reversing decisions made by the senior partner

- Refusal to accept constructive criticism
- Employee unrest
- Political maneuvering, as employees or managers form factions
- Severe reversal in financial position
- Increased service problems
- Loss of clients
- Lack of new business
- Loss of enthusiasm on the part of employees

When it becomes apparent that the time has come to part ways, you want to do it in the most civil manner possible. There's nothing to be gained from temper tantrums, recriminations, threats, or personal attacks. I will admit that this can be easier to recommend than to accomplish, but I urge you to try. Open and frank dialogue is imperative. There is no shame in admitting that it is just not working out. That doesn't mean there wasn't value in the time that preceded the break-up; it just means you have both reached a point where it makes sense to sever your partnership. If there are serious issues or breaches of trust involved, it is also prudent to build your case before trying to come to terms. Documented facts, such as letters, memos, or transcripts of telephone conversations, may be helpful if litigation or mediation comes into the picture. Not all partnerships end in a pleasant manner. Sometimes you have to be prepared for the worst.

Do not let these possibilities deter you from seeking a partnership. Having a major partner can help you grow your business, providing you choose the right partner and are prepared to do your part to keep the relationship strong and healthy. Collegial partnerships are fine, but it is important to reinforce the lines of authority regularly.

KEY LESSONS LEARNED

- Lines of responsibility and authority should be clearly defined
- Major partners should have complementary skills
- Partners should be compatible and share core values
- Use minority partnerships to motivate employees
- Partners can make the entrepreneurial experience more rewarding
- Open and honest communication is imperative for a successful partnership
- Recognize signs that things are not going well
- Try to end a partnership in a civil manner

CHAPTER EIGHT

YOU ARE YOUR OWN TALENT SCOUT

"Always treat your employees exactly as you would want them to treat your best customers."
— Stephen Covey

Having exceptional employees is the route to follow if you want your business to be successful. This is the one business axiom that will never change. The secret is to find them before your competitor does. Most entrepreneurs rely on standard recruiting methods such as advertisements or employment agencies to find new employees, but I'd like to recommend that you try what has worked for me for over 25 years. My system will take a little more effort on your part, but it will yield phenomenal results.

I am always on the lookout for talented people — anytime and any place. I may not have a specific position open, but that doesn't stop me from looking for great people. There's always room in my organization for the right person. If you are not already doing so, I would recommend that you start taking notice of the people around you at all times. I have hired people who

I met while sitting in an office or hotel lobby, buying something in a store, standing at the sign-in desk at a health club, and attending meetings. *Wherever there are people, there is the potential to find that special someone who just might be right for your company, now or in the future.*

When you get a chance to actually observe a person at work, you have the luxury of seeing them in their natural habitat. You get a feel for the way they handle their responsibilities, and often, you even get to see them interact with co-workers. Through this process, you gain a much clearer idea of their job-related abilities than you would in an interview situation, because you see them actually performing their job. In addition, there won't be the tension that is normally present during an interview, since the individual probably won't even be aware of what you are doing.

In October 2004, I was attending a convention in Newfoundland and was staying at the Fairmont. I chatted with one of the housekeeping staff members who cleaned my room and got to know her on a first-name basis. I was impressed with the way she approached her job and how personable she was. I learned that she and her husband owned a cleaning business in addition to their regular jobs. In turn, I told her about my Premiere Executive Suites company and said if she ever wanted a job, to give me a call.

In another example, I had seen Judy Sandor many times over a period of 15 years. She was in charge of guest services on the executive floor at the Dorval Hilton, where I was a regular guest. We had a number of conversations in the course of regular business, but one day I had the opportunity to observe her at her best. While I was waiting in the lounge, Judy had to handle two irate customers in a row, each with a different problem. Unfortunately for her, both of these gentlemen had worked up a head of steam before approaching her, and consequently she was the recipient of all of their pent-up anger and frustration. In spite of the unpleasantness of the situation, Judy handled each of them with diplomacy and grace. She was calm, collected, and soothing. She managed to defuse their anger and solve their problems simultaneously. Each of the guests went away satisfied. I felt compelled to tell her how impressed I was with the way she had conducted herself, and I filed this away in my memory bank. I immediately knew that she fit the profile of the type of person who would suit one of my businesses at some future date. Today, Judy is a partner and corporate salesperson with our Montreal franchise of Premiere Executive Suites.

Sometimes you meet people working in a totally different industry from your own, but you know instinctively they could easily transfer their skills to your business. Over the years, I have successfully recruited people who were already on one career path, but who had the potential to do well in one of my businesses. Included in this list have been teachers, bankers, Olympic athletes, and other professionals, who probably never expected to end up in either the moving or hospitality industries.

One total career changer was Clint Giffin in Halifax. Clint was an optician by profession, and had worked for two decades in that field. I first met him a number of years ago when I needed new glasses. I was referred to him by my friend and business partner in

Halifax, who told me he was the best in the business and that I shouldn't consider going anywhere else. I walked into his store without an appointment, and was greeted by this very personable, friendly gentleman who extended his hand to me and asked, "How may I help you?" From that first moment of contact, I was totally amazed by Clint's interpersonal skills, his unique radio announcer's type of voice, and how genuinely nice he was. The second time I came in to his store, I observed him with other customers. He was genuine and sincere in his desire to be of help to each of them. It was apparent to me that I had not received special treatment just because I had been referred to him. His interaction with every customer carried the same degree of care and attention. Obviously, this was the way he conducted himself at all times, and I was extremely impressed. When I took out my credit card to pay for my new glasses, I told him, "Clint, I think you are in the wrong business. You would do very well in the moving business. I really think you should consider joining our company." He told me politely but firmly that he had been an optician and a store manager for over 20 years, and that he had no plans to change careers. I wasn't deterred. We met several times before he finally decided to join us as a sales consultant. He has since become one of the most successful corporate sales representatives in the industry and is one of our senior partners in Halifax. Today, he will eagerly tell you how much he loves the business.

Every employee, regardless of function, is an important member of your team. However, if you were to ask me to name a job where it is critical to have the right person, I am likely to give you an unexpected answer.

To me, it is the job of receptionist. I honestly believe this is one of the most important positions in any company, yet too many businesspeople consider it just a junior or entry-level job. Nothing could be further from the truth. You know that you have a great receptionist when people start to make comments to you about this person. Everyone who calls in or comes to your company's office is a potential customer, so never underrate the value of that all-important first impression. A receptionist with a smile that comes through the telephone is invaluable to your organization. Contrarily, if that initial contact is with someone who is surly, unfriendly, unprofessional, or apathetic, the negative impression the caller gets is one that will stay with them, and will colour their perception about the entire company. The choice is yours: a great first impression or a bad first impression.

My advice would be to take a personal interest in who is hired for this important job. Again, I've been extremely fortunate over the years to have some truly extraordinary employees in this position. The first was Suzanne Bachur. She likes to tell people about her interview with me back in 1978. When I asked, "How fast can you type?" she responded, "I can't type very well, but I've got a smile, and I can answer the phone *really, really* well." Suzanne had the right attitude, and the dynamite personality needed for that position. When people spoke to Suzanne, they felt good, and that feeling carried over to their opinion about the company. Even if someone called with a complaint, having a friendly, helpful person deal with them first made them more at ease before they went on to speak to another member of our staff.

Another employee will always stand out in my memory as being an exceptional receptionist. Linda Pilon was someone I hired away from Nortel, after observing her on the job. It was a blend of personality and competence that impressed me, and made me determined to lure her away to work for my company. I suppose my client, Nortel, wasn't very happy about losing such a great employee, but their loss was certainly our gain. Two other fabulous receptionists who come to mind are Lisa Befrene, who worked in the Toronto office of my former moving company and now works with me at the new Premiere Van Lines office in Mississauga, and Cathy Siteman, who works at Premiere's Halifax office. Cathy answers the phone by saying, "Thank you for calling Premiere Executive Suites. My name is Cathy. How may I help you?" How's that for a welcome?

Along with making a great first impression, another mark of a truly gifted receptionist is the ability to recognize the voice of regular callers and to greet them by name before they identify themselves. Being able to do this is a great skill, and is a very valuable one for the company. Everyone likes to feel special, and when greeted in this manner by the receptionist the caller's mood and self-esteem are immediately elevated.

A great receptionist is also the one-person welcoming committee for visitors. Again, you want someone who is warm and pleasant. Visitors are then predisposed to like everyone else they encounter in the company. I've always stressed this point with our receptionists, and have made it a company policy for them to offer refreshments to the visitor regardless of who they are, and to engage them in some casual conversation.

This puts people at ease. I can recall a friend and business associate, Allan Church, commenting on the reception he received while waiting in our lobby. He said, "Tim, what *is* it about this place? This is the second time I've been here, and everyone is so friendly! Five employees passed through the waiting area, and each one took the time to stop and ask if there was anything they could do for me. I felt like I was a guest in someone's home, instead of just visiting an office."

Your receptionist is also a good source of information for the business owner. She knows everything that is going on in the company. She knows who is coming in late, taking long lunches, or leaving early. She knows who is not returning their calls (since people usually call back to complain) or who is abusing voice mail. You should make a point of meeting with your receptionist regularly to talk about these issues. Make sure, of course, she understands that you will never reveal where you heard anything specific, but let her know it is important that she share this kind of information with you for the good of the entire company.

One final point on the subject of receptionists: avoid the temptation to replace this position with one of those automated attendants that are available with phone systems today. Customers want to speak to a real person. What you save in salary will be lost ten times over when customers take their business to a competitor who understands that a receptionist is not someone who can be replaced by a computer.

As you can tell, I am very passionate when it comes to the topic of employees. Good employees will make you money either directly or indirectly through their efficiency and productivity. Don't make the mistake of settling for just a few star employees; instead, try to place outstanding people at every level, from the lowliest to the most senior manager. Collectively, you could well end up with a team of superstars, who will give you a real competitive advantage.

Another place you really need superstars is your sales team. Over the years, I have hired many such individuals. One that stands out in my mind, perhaps because I have recently had the opportunity to hire him for a second time, is Frank Martin. Years ago, my partner Barry Stanton (who was the branch manager of our flagship office in Mississauga) and I hired Frank. We saw that he had incredible potential, and he certainly didn't let us down. He became a million-dollar producer, putting him in the top echelon of salespeople in the moving industry. Frank was diligent, honest, hardworking, and a great communicator. When I was assembling a team for my new moving company, Premiere Van Lines, someone mentioned Frank's name and told me he might be interested in joining the new firm. Although I hadn't seen him in awhile, I remembered how well respected he was by his peers and how hard he worked. When the opportunity presented itself, I offered him a job with the new company and I am happy to say he accepted it.

Generally, I make it a practice to include others in my hiring decisions, since I firmly believe it is important for new staff members to fit in with existing employees. Therefore, in addition to myself, I usually have three different people interview a candidate before a final hiring decision is reached. For a workplace to operate effectively, it is imperative that all (or at least many) employees get along with others in the company. Everything functions better when people like and respect their co-workers. A strong degree of cooperation among peers, and a lack of conflict, is what you want to strive for, regardless of the size of your operation.

Another hiring tip is to understand that it is not necessary to hire people — especially managers — who are a clone of yourself. In fact, it makes more sense to hire people with a variety of skills and talents in order to provide your company with more depth. At the same time, it is important that all employees and managers share a common vision with you about the company. It is therefore imperative for you to share your vision with them, not just once, when they are hired, but on a regular basis to reinforce it in their minds. You cannot shirk this responsibility. In his bestselling book, *Leaders Must Lead*, author John Burdell put it this way: "To touch people's hearts is to involve them in the decisions that impact their lives. To keep them informed beyond what they need to know and provide an answer to the ever present question, *What's in it for me?*"

Have regular meetings to share recent company successes, or discuss problems or issues in casual, one-on-one conversations as you walk around your office or operational headquarters. I have found that I sometimes get incredibly important information during these walkabouts. One of my former employees, Gary Kofoed, sent me a note when I left the moving company in 1999 to tell me how grateful he was for our little chats over the years. He wrote that they made him feel involved, and that the genuine interest I displayed in his work and in his life helped to motivate him. Gary's decades-long record as a top producing salesperson is proof that the time spent was very worthwhile, and does have measurable results.

Reaching out to your employees and making them understand you care about them as human beings is one of the things that sets great leaders apart from mediocre ones. At a recent human resources conference held in Toronto, the keynote speaker, Tim Saunders from Yahoo! Inc., told a very dramatic story during his address that was titled, "The Compassionate Leader." Tim was discussing how impersonal today's workplace has become, where people sitting in the next cubicle will send an email to their co-worker rather than get up and walk three feet to talk to them. In workplaces like this, many managers have virtually no contact with their employees other than by memo or email. Tim told the story of one such company where productivity was slipping and so the senior manager decided to get some professional advice. What was suggested was very simple but foreign to the way this manager felt a business should be run. It was recommended that he get in the habit of walking around the office each day, stopping to talk to his employees in a casual one-on-one basis. While the idea made him a little uncomfortable, the manager agreed to try it.

And so commenced his daily walkabouts. Before long, he started telling his employees some personal things about his life. One such revelation to a young, rather nerdy fellow who shared the manager's love of all things electronic was that his wife didn't want him to buy the latest X-Box since she felt it was a waste of money.

Soon, the atmosphere around the office changed, employees were happier, and productivity was up. The manager was pleased. One day he got a surprise visit from the same shy young man with whom he had shared the story about the X-Box. The young man came bearing a wrapped gift that he presented with a flourish. The manager opened the gift to find an X-Box. He was flabbergasted. "I can't accept this," he said. "It's far too expensive. Why on earth would you purchase such a gift for me?" The young fellow replied, "I got this for you with the money I got from selling my gun. You see, I had been planning to kill myself. That's why I bought the gun in the first place. Each night I would go home and practice putting the barrel in my mouth, trying to get up the courage to really do it. I felt I had nothing to live for. But then you started coming by my desk every day just to say hi and ask how things were going. You asked me about what I liked to do in my spare time, if I liked my job, and what the company could do to make things better for me. You really seemed to care. That's when I decided not to kill myself."

Well, I can tell you there wasn't a dry eye in the room after that story. I'm sure many managers went back to their office after the conference with a plan to start paying more personal attention to their employees.

When asked, employees who are dissatisfied with their jobs will tell you that lack of communication is one of the things they find most frustrating. It is hard to be an ambassador for your company if you don't clearly understand what the company stands for, and where the owner/manager wants to take it. Most people want to be part of a company they feel an affinity for, and one they are proud of. However, if the owner/manager never shares information with them, then they feel disconnected. Unfortunately, this sometimes leads to a sense of apathy. I have always made it a point to share information about the company with my employees, both in good times and bad.

Sharing confidential information with employees can lead to greater loyalty and a higher degree of commitment. You might be very surprised at what your employees are prepared to do to help the company thrive, and even to survive. Rather than you having to be heavy-handed, when it is necessary to reduce costs, your employees might offer to make some sacrifices and accept short-term pain to help the company through a difficult period. I have experienced this first-hand, on more than one occasion.

One such time occurred when I was trying to buy out my first partner. I knew the company would be better off with him gone, but I was having a hard time raising the money. You can imagine my surprise when one of my employees, Barbara Cochrane, offered to mortgage her home in order to give me some money. I didn't take her up on her offer, but I've never forgotten that generous gesture.

Employees who are treated well will reward you with hard work, dedication, and loyalty. They will genuinely care about the company. I believe that when employees are made to feel they are special, they rise to the occasion and consciously choose to become special. Good people become great, and great people become extraordinary. The group begins to feed off each other's energy and competence. This attitude is then displayed to everyone they are exposed to, including clients, co-workers, suppliers, and competitors. Before you know it, people are talking about what a great place your company is to work. What more could any employer want?

One ingredient of a distinctive corporate culture is

the presence of a sense of fun. I don't subscribe to the theory that business has to be serious and boring. You can be serious about business and still have fun. I have never been able to understand managers who chastise or discipline employees for talking to each other, or joking around a little in the office. I have visited some offices that are like a morgue. No wonder the employees look depressed and unhappy! What is wrong with a little enjoyment, as long as the work is done? I recommend that you encourage your employees to laugh together — not just at an annual company function, but on a daily basis. When you consider that you spend at least one-third of your life at work, it only makes sense that you should enjoy being there. Unhappy employees have negative attitudes and are generally less productive than happy employees.

A recent study done by Towers Perrin measured the cost of negative employees. It found that disengaged employees cost employer corporations $27.7 billion in Canada and $350 billion in the United States — staggering numbers that give food for thought. The study asked employees to rank what they needed to feel fully engaged at their jobs. The results were:

1. Exciting work challenge
2. Career growth and development
3. Great people and a fun environment
4. Fair pay
5. A good boss

I once read a statistic that said the average adult laughs approximately five times per day, while a child may laugh some 200 times! Laughter is good from both a physiological and psychological perspective. There's nothing wrong with being a little silly with your co-workers. As an example, at a recent convention for all of Premiere Executive Suites' partners and employees, we had a group hug — and in public, no less! It might sound corny, but it made us all feel really good, and when we got down to work, we accomplished a lot.

Another interesting statistic that came up in several recent studies showed that people who laugh and are happy at their jobs have a lower absentee rate. Also, employees who laugh together are usually more capable of solving on-the-job disputes in a sensible manner than those who are disconnected from their co-workers.

If you want to create a happy and productive workplace, then I would recommend you do your best to foster a spirit of camaraderie among your employees. Have potluck lunches, barbeques, or other casual events. Celebrate birthdays, anniversaries, retirements, and other milestones in their lives. These occasions will give your employees opportunities to get to know each other on a personal level, and that leads to a better working relationship.

Finding the right employees and then treating them well is one of the easiest ways to build a successful business.

KEY LESSONS LEARNED

- Seeing people in their natural working environment is more informative than spending time in a regular interview
- Always be on the lookout for future employees wherever you go
- Look for exceptional employees to fill as many positions as possible
- Committed employees make money for the company or can save it money
- Share your vision with employees
- Communicate with employees on a regular basis
- Create a fun working environment

CHAPTER NINE

LEADING THE TROOPS TO THE TOP OF THE MOUNTAIN

"A leader takes people where they want to go. A great leader takes people where they don't think they can go and shows them the way."
— *Rosalynn Carter*

As a business owner, it is your job to assemble the best team of employees that you can. As their leader, you have to help them reach their full potential. Your next challenge is to *keep* those employees by providing them challenges and rewards so they never want to leave. At the same time, this is not a one-way street. Employees have to understand that they must work hard and earn their place on the winning team. Once people are part of a high-performing team, they will want to maintain this status. **Being part of an elite group does a lot for an individual's self-esteem, and this is especially true if the calibre of the team is widely recognized outside of the company.**

I've been fortunate to see this happen numerous times throughout my career. I can remember one occasion when a North American Van Lines senior executive came up to Canada to attend a regional meeting. There were several hundred people present at the conference, and yet it was our people who drew this man's attention. He said he could pick our people out in the crowd, because they all radiated "a special something." He said their appearance was part of it; they were better dressed and more professional looking. However, it was more about the way they acted. He said our people all appeared confident, enthusiastic, respectful, and comfortable making conversation with others. He also commented on the fact that our employees took every opportunity to promote our company without appearing boastful or arrogant. And then he put the icing on the cake when he said he couldn't help noticing how the members of our group seemed to have genuine affection for each other. He said this was a rare thing in the business world. I can't begin to tell you how proud I was of our employees, after hearing this assessment from a man whose position led him to meet thousands of people each year.

A similar thing happened to me more recently with my Premiere Executive Suites' partners and staff. We had a friend of mine, Tom Vincent, address our group about the challenges of the accommodations industry. Tom works for Bridgestreet, the second largest extended-stay firm in the world, and is one of the real pioneers in the business. I have a great deal of respect for him and his opinions. After spending just a few hours with our group, he said to me, "I can't believe the quality of people that you have working for Premiere, Tim. You have assembled an amazing group!" It was evident he had identified that combination of positive attitude, confidence, attractiveness, and happiness that permeates our entire team.

Motivating people is an important part of creating a successful business. Robert Waterman Jr. and Tom Peters, in their classic business study *In Search of Excellence*, identified five key motivating factors:

1. **Control:** People need a sense of control over their jobs. Empower your employees. I learned early on in my career not to micro-manage. Instead, I tell my employees what is expected of them and then I give them the authority to make their own decisions. Even when those decisions are wrong, I back them up.

2. **Belief:** People must believe in the company and what it stands for.

   This is where communication is key. I've always made it a practice to share my vision about the company and its core values. Our employees know what our standards are and respect our commitment to maintain them at all times.

3. **Challenge:** People need to be challenged. Don't let them coast.

   I make a point of hiring the best people available, but I make it clear to them that they cannot rest on the laurels of their past reputation. I have high expectations. I believe that people need to be challenged to exceed their goals. They know they must achieve these goals in order to remain on the team. I find this approach ignites their competitive spirit.

4. **Learning:** People need the opportunity to improve their skills. Encourage this.

   I'm a big believer in ongoing professional development. I encourage employees to take courses, read business books, and network with experts. Learning should be a life-long pursuit.

5. Recognition: People need to feel appreciated. Praise them often.

> This is an area that many entrepreneurs don't pay enough attention to. You must make this a priority. Recognition can be as simple as telling employees they are doing a great job. In addition, you should find ways to offer public recognition or provide rewards for exceptional performance.

To be a great leader, your people must trust you. Lack of trust is one thing you don't want present in your company. It will undermine everything you are trying to accomplish.

In business today, there is a credibility gap between employers and employees. As Jim Clemmer, author of *Going the Distance*, says, "Credibility is based on a perception of trustworthiness, reliability, and integrity." According to recent studies, only 53% of employees believe what they hear from senior management. *Give your employees, clients, and suppliers reason to trust you by making your word your bond.* Don't go back on your word, even if you regret making a particular decision or promise.

Another way to gain trust is to *be consistent in your approach to decisions, problems, and discipline.* Don't be erratic. There's nothing employees hate more than not knowing "which boss" will turn up on any given day. Some refer to this unpleasant situation as "the good boss" and "the bad boss." The same thing goes for blatant favouritism. It's only human nature to like certain people more than others. However, in business, you must make every effort to treat all employees fairly. Otherwise, you are setting the stage for problems.

Resentment will build, productivity will decline, and negativity will take over.

Here are three ideas to keep trust alive and well in your workplace:

1. **Communicate:** Keep employees informed, explain decisions, and be honest about problems.

2. **Support:** Remember that employees are people. Show concern when they have problems, be approachable, and encourage and coach them.

3. **Respect:** Be respectful of employees' opinions, listen to them, never discipline them in public, and never use foul language with them.

I also feel that you should encourage every employee in your organization to have a sales mentality. If they feel good about the company and believe in it, they will want to recommend the company's product or services to their family and friends. Consider paying them a small commission for referrals that turn into sales. It provides a little additional incentive and is a good motivator. I've always done this, and it has worked out well. Harvey MacKay, of the highly successful MacKay Envelope Company, made a similar point in his witty and important book, *Swim with the Sharks*. He was asked how many salespeople he had in his firm, and his answer was "350." Then, he was asked how many *employees* he had, and, once again, his answer was "350." All companies should be so lucky.

Motivating your employees is only one side of the equation. You can create a fabulous workplace and offer all the incentives in the world, but if your employees don't do their part then all is lost. Employees also have a responsibility to produce results and pay their way if they expect to retain their jobs. I believe that *every person in the company must do their part to make the firm successful.* How you measure those results depends on the position. Obviously, it is easier to measure the contribution made by salespeople and managers, but it is also possible to do the same for employees who perform other functions in your business. The first step in making employees accountable is to let them know what criteria will be used to measure their performance. There should be some type of quantitative formula used to provide you with accurate information. For example:

- Managers are expected to turn a profit of 8–12%

- Sales managers must lead by example. So, 70–80% of their time should be devoted to developing business, and no more than 30% of their time should be devoted to sales administration matters

- Sales personnel should be given specific sales targets, on a monthly, quarterly, and annual basis. Bonuses should be part of the remuneration package for exceeding targets. Sales costs should not exceed 10–11% (i.e. If sales are $500,000 then the total employee cost to company should be in the $50,000 range)

Establish some form of bench-marking that is quantifiable and fair. This brings me to a discussion of a concept that may not be popular but can be effective. For years I had an informal approach to culling weak team members. Each year I would terminate the bottom

Tim, in jersey #34, with his basketball team at Michael Power High School (late 1960s)

Tim receives a basketball trophy at Michael Power High School, Toronto, Ontario (late 1960s)

Tim at St. Augustine's Seminary, Scarborough, Ontario (late 1960s)

TC Moore Transport truck, Montreal, Quebec (mid 1970s)

Tim's 1985 Rolls Royce Corniche with his mother's name on the vanity licence plates

Tim with his 1960 Silver Cloud Rolls Royce that came with a home he bought in the mid 1980s

Tim on a parasailing trip (mid 1980s)

Tim's eldest sons, Tim Jr. and Jason (1989)

PARTNERSHIPS

IN FOR THE LONG HAUL

Adding new partners as he's expanded his moving business has given Tim Moore what he needs to take on his larger rivals: management strength and money

BY GERRY BLACKWELL

"I know my strengths," says Tim Moore in his jock-philosopher tone, "and I know my weaknesses." Judging by Moore's achievements, his strengths generally cancel out the weaknesses. In just 10 years he has built AMJ Campbell Van Lines Inc. from a $250,000 local household mover to a profitable $50-million operation with 32 branches across the country. Based in Mississauga, Ont., AMJ's revenues have grown by a minimum of 22% each year since Moore bought the Atlas Van Lines/Canada Ltd. agency in 1977.

A flamboyant entrepreneur who sports Italian designer suits and burgundy snakeskin boots, and who drives a cherry-

Moore leads "by virtue of his charisma, his style," according to one of his marketing vice-presidents, Jackie Stewart. Moore believes that the best way to run a company is to spread the wealth—and the responsibility—around. To find the stuff willing to take up this challenge, "I look for the personality first," says Moore, "the sincerity, the integrity, the philosophy of life."

Finding good employees is one of the ways Moore compensates for his impatience with administrative details and his penchant for lavish spending. He looks for people who can do what he can't or doesn't want to do. Bonding key employ-

May 1989 *Canadian Business* magazine article on Tim and AMJ Campbell Van Lines

Terry and Tim Moore on a heli-hiking trip in Bugaboos, British Columbia (2001)

Tim and his wife Bernardine on a heli-hiking trip in Bugaboos, British Columbia (2001)

Tim and Lyn Leal of Premiere Van Lines Calgary (bottom row, second from left) with their "Snow Hosting Group," Sunshine Village, Banff, Alberta (2002)

With Senator Donald Oliver, Honourable Lieutenant Governor of Nova Scotia Myra Freeman, and her husband Larry, Tim receives a Queen's Golden Jubilee Medal (2003)

Tim and Bernardine at the Crane Resort, Barbados (2003)

Tim on his motorcycle tour of Newfoundland (2004)

Tim, Mike Flynn, Lisa, and David Reid on their motorcycle tour of Newfoundland (2004)

Tim's birthday party, December, 2004. From top left: Judy Moore, Lyn Moore, Lynn Moore, Amy Jarvis, Carol Davis, Bernardine Moore, Tatiana Kredl, Jackie Stewart, Ann Moore, Tim Moore, and Judy Sandor

Tim and Bernardine with Ron Joyce (cofounder of Tim Hortons) on his $50 million sailboat, Barbados (2004)

Tim's house in Chester,
Nova Scotia

An aerial view of Tim's
house in Chester,
Nova Scotia

From top left: Matthew, Christopher, Bernardine, and Tim Moore with Bernadine's mother, Rita Bohan (2004)

Suzanne Bachur, Executive Vice President, Premiere Executive Suites (2004)

Former AMJ boss behind the wheel of rival firm

Tim Moore was owner and president of AMJ Campbell, Canada's biggest independent moving van line, until he retired in 1998. But now he's returning to the business to head a group of former AMJ franchisees who, disgruntled with new management, are launching a rival company. **B8**

"Moving you Home" VAN LINES

30 Offices Coast to Coast

THE GLOBE AND MAIL

CANADA'S NATIONAL NEWSPAPER • FOUNDED 1844 • GLOBEANDMAIL.COM • MONDAY, FEBRUARY 7, 2005

B8 · CANADIAN BUSINESS

TRUCKING

New van line aims to drive AMJ off road

Tim Moore owned and ran AMJ Campbell until retiring. Now he's back to help disgruntled former franchisees launch a rival van line.

SANDOR FIZLI/THE GLOBE AND MAIL

Irked ex-franchisees recruit former CEO

BY GORDON PITTS

Tim Moore spent two decades building **AMJ Campbell Inc.** from a tiny van line into Canada's biggest independent mover. But now he wants to run his old company off the road.

Mr. Moore, whose ties to Mississauga-based AMJ Campbell were severed in a bitter legal battle two years ago, is launching rival **Premiere Van Lines**, a company built on dissident former AMJ Campbell franchisees.

But this is not a story of revenge, insisted Mr. Moore, 60, who is moving to Toronto from his retirement home in Chester, N.S., to command the new national enterprise. "I had to come back and give back my support to this group [of franchisees]," said Mr. Moore, adding that Premiere will hit the ground running with 17 branches and close to $40-million in annual revenue.

"It is the franchise guys who are driving it, and they have come to Tim to lead them," said Daryl Amirault, a Halifax-area franchise owner acting as Premiere president until Mr. Moore takes over officially April 1 when the firm hits the road.

Mr. Amirault, a business partner of Mr. Moore, said the relationship between AMJ head office and local franchises deteriorated under current AMJ president Bruce Bowser.

Mr. Bowser, once Mr. Moore's protégé, denied there was a widespread revolt against his leadership, but acknowledges Mr. Moore's new company will be a competitor in the national moving industry. He said the exodus of franchisees—14 in all, he said—would not hurt his company's ability to serve the 38 Canadian cities where it now operates through about 55 branches.

He said disgruntled franchisees are mainly a group to whom AMJ Campbell had decided not to offer renewals as their long-term contracts approached maturity on March 31. The plan was to convert a number of these branches to company-owned operations or to enlist new franchisees, he said.

He denied Mr. Moore's contention that AMJ Campbell, which has annual revenue of more than $100-million, has offered financial inducements to lure some defectors back in the system.

Mr. Browser also disputed Premiere's claims that it will immedi-

ately gross $40-million a year, making it the second-largest Canadian mover behind either AMJ or another rival firm. He said a reorganized AMJ Campbell will maintain its current levels of business in the cities where the companies compete.

But Mr. Moore insisted that "you cannot replace infrastructure and the talents and character of this group. This group clearly represents the culture of the moving company that made us famous."

The dispute has been brewing for some time. Flamboyant Mr. Moore gained a high profile as the owner and president of AMJ Campbell, which grew dramatically as Canadian agent for Atlas Van Lines. He wrote a book about his experiences—*On the Move: How to Survive and Succeed as an Entrepreneur.*

Having sold AMJ in 1988, he came back as CEO in 1991 to help guide it through hard times. But by the late 1990s, Mr. Moore had retreated from day-to-day management, and tapped Mr. Bowser as the next president. Mr. Moore settled into a semi-retired consulting role at a salary of $150,000 a year.

Mr. Moore began to be critical of

Mr. Bowser's management style, and wrote a letter to his successor in 2002 alleging that the new president was undermining the chain's collegial culture. Those allegations were also made by franchisees who had been close to Mr. Moore.

In November, 2002, AMJ Campbell was the target of a takeover attempt led by Halifax investor George Armoyan. Mr. Moore has denied allegations he was involved in the bid. The moving company was ultimately acquired by a management group led by Mr. Bowser.

In December, 2002, Mr. Moore's consulting contract was ended, and the former president sued his old company for breach of contract. The suit was resolved out of court.

The dissident franchisees approached Mr. Moore a year ago about helping them, Mr. Amirault says, but the former president was restrained by a non-compete agreement until Oct. 1. About two months ago, Mr. Moore said, he decided to get back in the moving business. "My intent was only to go back and help a few people out. What has happened is everybody is jumping on the bandwagon."

PROFIT

YOUR GUIDE TO BUSINESS SUCCESS

Sell More!

How the masters made their greatest sales

Steal the secrets of **10** master sellers as they share the lessons of their most memorable sales

Tim Moore
President and CEO, Premiere Van Lines, Toronto, and Premiere Executive Suites, Halifax; founder, AMJ Campbell Van Lines, Toronto

Executive Suites. But about a year ago, 17 AMJ franchisees got together and asked me to meet with them. What happened next—in my presentation in November in the Marriott Hotel in Toronto—was my finest sales moment.

I went into the meeting with an objective of talking to them from the heart. I wanted to congratulate them on their courage in resolving through the process, and to sell them on the idea of a new vision.

I outlined the plan to them. I would run the company for a two-year period, and then be chairman for five years. The company, I suggested, would be commercially owned. I talked about quality of service. I talked

about things like adopting full uniforms, including ties, and insisting on quality-assurance reports. "We are here for one reason," I told them, "and it's to service our customer." I said I would be relentless with this.

I was selling a value system in that meeting. I was selling the idea of the core group coming back together with a culture of respect—which is one of the things that made AMJ famous. I was selling open communication, affection and friendship. I was calling change.

When I left the room that days, I knew in my heart that I was back in the moving business, even though I really did not want to go back into the moving business.

Afterward, I heard how people felt. They were below, but after them, they were moved about what they wanted to go. I track record management. You. And I was able those things that important to integrity and They were able what's clock is for people do well.

Our new paperback off Premiere Execly called Van Lines. We are panies constant success of Sales emise. Suddsecond-large party in Ca

PREMIERE
"Moving you Home" VAN LINES

Premiere Van Lines comes to life

BY KATE CHANDLER
BUSINESS TIMES

ST. CATHARINES — April 1, 2005 will mark the beginning of a new chapter for Leo Thibodeau's St. Catharines-based moving company. For the past 11 years, Thibodeau and his partner Terri Lynn Dixon have been franchisees of Canada's largest coast-to-coast moving company. Along with 16 other former-franchisees, they're breaking out on their own and forming what could potentially be Canada's second largest moving company, Premiere Van Lines.

"Our customers have a right to know we've changed our operating name and we've changed it so we can continue doing business as we have for the last 11 years," said Thibodeau.

He is excited about forming a partnership with like-minded businesses across Canada to provide the highest level of service to their customers from coast-to-coast. As an Atlas Van Lines agent, Premiere Van Lines will have

in every province and territory in Canada.

"We're not franchisees any longer, we're partners," he added.

The St. Catharines location has expanded its territory and now included everywhere from Fort Erie to Hamilton, where it used to end at Beamsville. It is also establishing a commercial office division in Mississauga.

"It's certainly an opportunity for us here," said Thibodeau. "It's allowed us the opportunity to expand our market and become involved in other divisions."

As the company has been developed over the past few months, Darryl Amirault of Halifax, Nova Scotia has been the interim president. On April 1, Tim Moore, founder of AMJ Van Lines, will step into Amirault's shoes and take a leadership role in the company.

"The structure of Premiere is obviously still in the works," said Thibodeau. "One major difference for us will

Many of the companies that have partnered in Premiere Van Lines, have been ranked as some of the top quality service providers in the country and together they are expected to have revenues of about $40 million, according to Thibodeau.

The 20 locations have a couple hundred vehicles and employees and they expect to grow considerably as Premiere.

"Our company's going to grow here," noted Thibodeau. "It provides growth opportunities we've never really been afforded."

About four months ago, Premiere Van Lines was just an idea and since then, it has taken the efforts of many people to bring it to life.

"We realistically didn't have much time at all to put (the company) together," he said. "It's happening because of the support from our customers and our employees. They're embracing the change willingly and accepting it with open

...ion, call 905-

A6   Thursday, April 7, 2005   The Chronicle Herald
Special Advertising Feature

The Birth of Canada's Newest National Moving Company!

PREMIERE VAN LINES
"EXCELLENCE IN MOVING"   Atlas Van Lines

468-4313
www.premierevanlines.com

New national mover offering customer-focused service

Premiere Van Lines delivering the most moving experience possible

By Irene Thomas
Special Features Writer

Premiere Van Lines is a new national moving company with a mission of delivering the best customer-focused service possible.

"Premiere Van Lines is a multi-branch national moving company which serves all of Canada," explains Premiere Van Lines' Halifax branch partner and vice-president of sales Clint Giffin.

"Multi-branch means that consumers receive a continuity of communication and service levels from coast to coast.

"Simply put, continuity of communication means you know that the same people who begin your move are the same ones you deal with at the end of your move."

The piece of mind Premiere Van Lines offers its clients means the consumer rights and their valuable possessions are fully protected.

In Metro Halifax, Premiere Van Lines is located at 31 John Savage Avenue in the Burnside Industrial Park. Across Atlantic Canada, the professional moving company has offices in Sydney, Truro, Moncton, Saint John, Fredericton and St. John's.

Premiere Van Lines is also an agent for Atlas Van Lines in Canada and the United States.

"Van line affiliation is critical," says Giffin. "Premiere Van Lines ensures you, the customer, that a certain code of ethics and levels of service must be met in order to maintain an agent status with Atlas Van Lines."

When asked why people should choose Premiere Van Lines to be their mover, Giffin says the company, as its name implies, offers premiere service at competitive rates.

"We employ people who share our common goals and values. We believe in integrity, fairness and friendship. With that common vision, Premiere Van Lines delivers the most moving experience possible," says Giffin.

"Continuity of communication means you know that the same people who begin your move are the same ones you deal with at the end of your move."
Clint Giffin
Branch partner
vice-president sales
Premiere Van Lines

Premiere Van Lines is a multibranch national moving company which serves all of Canada.

Clint Giffin, partner and vice president, sales, Premiere Van Lines: "We believe in integrity, fairness and friendship."

The entire Premiere Van Lines Group (2005)

Premiere Van Lines Board of Directors. Top row: Walt Peniuk, Joe Bourdreau, Garth Richards, and Darryl Amirault. Bottom row: Mike Savoy, Michael Warnick, Jackie Stewart, and Tim Moore (2005)

Premiere Executive Suites partners. Back row: Lois Roque, Terry Moore, Diane Jones-Konihowski, Dave Blackman, and Tim Moore. Front row: Kim Boydell, Judy Sandor, Tatiana Kredl, and Barbara Murphy (2005)

Mayor Hazel McCallion and Tim (2005)

Pope Benedict XVI, Archbishop Daniel Bohan, Bernardine and Tim Moore (2005)

10% of employees. Of course, I always had talks with those who were not carrying their weight, and gave them sufficient opportunity to improve. I provided specific suggestions and always documented these discussions. It is a point of pride for me that I've never been sued for wrongful dismissal. People who are not a good fit with a company usually know it and may actually appreciate your candor. Now, before you begin to think that I am some kind of tyrant, please realize that my approach is common practice in some of North America's largest corporations, including General Electric and Ford. In fact, until a few years ago, this practice was a stated corporate objective at these larger corporations. More recently, because of changes in business philosophy — and, in some cases, labour laws — these companies have made it less of a mandate.

One way or another, most major corporations evaluate their employees' performance to determine who should stay and who should go. Donald Trump's highly successful television show, "The Apprentice," has made a cult saying out of the phrase, "You're fired!" That being said, I can tell you in all honesty that I have never experienced one moment of pleasure out of having to let someone go. I've always tried to be as constructive and sensitive as possible in these situations. But it's just a fact of life that some people won't meet your standards or fit into your corporate culture. When this happens, it is usually best to let them go before they become a disruptive influence in your workplace.

When an employee's performance isn't satisfactory, it is important to take the time to sit down with the employee and let them know what needs improvement. Specific skills, work ethic, attitude, an inability to meet goals, or any combination of these may be targeted. Always be specific in regards to the problem area. Get the employee to agree to a course of action to rectify the situation, and set a deadline for improvement. Then follow up these discussions with a letter that documents what was discussed and agreed to. Keep the tone of the letter as positive as possible, but make sure all the pertinent facts are included.

Up until the point that a person leaves the company, you should never stop trying to motivate them. If a person is salvageable, then by all means do what you can to help. It is an expensive proposition to retrain a replacement employee, but is sometimes your only option. Always remember, here in Canada it is very important to build and document a case, should it become necessary to fire someone. People should always be given an opportunity to turn things around, but if the situation doesn't improve, then follow through and let them go. Don't procrastinate, since doing so only makes it harder on everyone.

Another cause for dismissal, in my opinion, is an employee's lack of respect for their fellow employees or their manager. People who have a bad attitude or are abusive to others have no place in the workplace.

At the same time, it is important not to totally destroy someone when you fire them. Be sensitive to the situation; take time to mention their good points, but tell them that it just isn't working for the company, and let them leave with dignity. I abhor the practice some businesspeople have of firing someone, then humiliating them in front of their peers. I know of situations where a person was given virtually no notice, and was escorted out of the building by a security guard. Unless you have a serious case of financial malfeasance, or a highly violent individual, such actions are totally inappropriate, as well as inhuman. If someone was good enough to have been your employee for a period of time, then they are good enough to be permitted to leave with dignity.

I realize that my use of this culling concept may sound contrary to my prior comments about the importance of employee motivation. But, frankly, poor performers drag down the entire team, and other team members often begin to resent the poor-performing individual. High-performing people are generally self-motivating individuals — but not always. I can recall several times when certain staff members would come into my office and sit in my chair. They would tell me that they would like to be in my position, and be the boss. My comment would always be the same: "Hey, I don't have a problem with that. You just have to earn it." I have seen some of the most talented individuals squander their potential, simply because they weren't willing to work hard enough or to make a few sacrifices. You have to make it clear to your employees what you expect of them, and let them know there will be consequences if they don't give it their best effort.

As you can see by the advice offered in this chapter, *leading and nurturing employees is time-consuming work.* But I can assure you, it's worth it. With a team of hard-working, dedicated employees, your business is well on its way to being a successful venture.

Congratulations!

KEY LESSONS LEARNED

- Assemble — and keep — the best possible team of employees
- Empower your employees; help them to believe in the firm; challenge them to do their best
- Give everyone associated with your company good reason to trust you
- Be consistent in all your approaches to problems, discipline, and decision-making
- Every person in your company is a potential salesperson
- Make employees accountable for performance
- Ensure employees understand how their performance will be measured
- Let weak employees go, but let them leave with dignity intact

CHAPTER TEN

THINK OUTSIDE
THE BOX

"Creativity is thinking up new things. Innovation is doing new things."
— *Theodore Levitt*

One of the biggest challenges facing new entrepreneurs is finding ways to get noticed in today's crowded marketplace. If money were no object, then the answer would be simple: simply flood the print, radio, and TV media with advertisements. Throw in billboards all over the city, and you're bound to get noticed. Unfortunately, this approach is not an option for most entrepreneurs, especially new ones. (The many thousands of dollars it costs for even quarter-page ads in major newspapers may shock you.) There are options, but like everything else of value, it means a little more work on your part.

With so many businesses trying to attract the attention of consumers, you have to give some serious thought to this subject *before* you embark on a new business. This is why choosing the right business in the first place is so critical. It is rare to have a truly unique product or service, and even if you do find such an opportunity, it won't be long before it, too, has competition. A successful entrepreneur understands that *getting noticed ahead of the competition is a never-ending race.*

I recommend that aspiring entrepreneurs consider a *service type of business* over a product-based one. We live in a relationship era and a service business is all about establishing and maintaining client relationships. A business that offers a highly personal type of service, whereby you have extensive interaction with your customer, is ideal. I've always believed that the closer you can get to your customer (and by you, I mean you and all of your employees), the higher your chances are for success. A business that has a mix of corporate and consumer clientele also offers you additional marketing opportunities. I also believe it is somewhat easier to create points of difference through service enhancements, or value-added benefits.

Obviously, a lot depends on the type of business you have chosen. As aspiring entrepreneurs, most of you will not have access to huge amounts of capital, and will be considering the kinds of small businesses that won't require a large initial capital outlay. As for your future, some of you will be satisfied to start small, and gradually build up your business to the point where it provides a comfortable lifestyle. Others may be thinking ahead to the day when they can expand into additional locations, franchise their business, or even go public. Regardless of how modest or how aggressive your goals are, the process is the same. And one key step in that process is making your business stand out in a crowded marketplace. It's not easy, but it *can* be done.

What can you do to get your company noticed, and

better yet, talked about? How can you get your company's name out in the public domain, when you don't have a big advertising budget? For starters, look for ways to get your name in the media — and this does not always have to be through paid advertising. Everything going on in your company should be publicly promoted. If you've won an award, opened a new office, hired a star employee (especially someone with a stellar track record), then tell the world. When we brought Olympian Diane Jones-Konihowski on as a partner in Premiere Executive Suites, we made a point of calling the newspapers. Naturally, they were interested in doing a story on this high profile woman who was embarking on a totally new career.

Hiring well-known people is a very smart move for any company. Don't immediately assume they won't be interested in joining your firm. If your company is an exciting place to work, you might be very surprised to see who would be interested in joining your team. Former athletes are often looking for new career opportunities when they are ready to move on from the world of sports. Many of them have spent years making sacrifices and are ready to enter the world of business so they too can make some decent money. I have had a great deal of success doing this over the years. Most athletes already have the work ethic, determination, and commitment to do whatever is necessary to succeed. Who better to have on your team?

As an alternative to hiring former athletes full time, you can look into sponsorship opportunities as we did with people like curler Russ Howard, rower Silken Laumann, and speed skaters Catriona Le May Doan and Jeremy Witherspoon. My brother's company in

Calgary is currently working with Jeremy as he continues to pursue his sports career.

The important thing about getting noticed is you have to keep your name out there if you want to do better than your competitors. One way is to approach a staff writer on a local paper with a story idea: What is there about your business that might appeal to readers? Is there some unique aspect to the service or product you offer? Is there a human-interest element to something directly related with your business, or with something you've done for your community? Don't forget that, just as you are always looking for customers, reporters are always looking for a new story to share with their readers. In 2003, we were able to interest *Profit* magazine in doing an article on Premiere Executive Suites. The result was a four-page article plus photographs in the national magazine.

Stories centred around charitable efforts, including the donations of services in kind or fundraising done for a community organization, are always well received. For example, a number of years ago, there was a serious flood in Winnipeg. The banks of the Assiniboine River were overflowing, and hundreds of houses were either under water or seriously damaged. My brother Terry, who was based in Calgary, initiated a relief effort by involving other companies in Alberta. Together, they brought resources into Manitoba to help the people who had been flooded out of their homes. Terry supplied trucks and manpower to deliver furniture, clothing, and other household effects that had been donated by people in Alberta. Money was also raised from numerous corporations to help displaced people get their lives back in order. Helping these people at such a difficult time was truly appreciated by the entire community, and the publicity created for our company was overwhelming.

More recently, our Halifax franchisee spent days helping victims after Hurricane Juan swept through Nova Scotia. I know our people would be willing to help during any disaster, with or without public recognition. However, good works usually do garner some positive publicity, so it really becomes a win-win situation for the company, which gets its name, and perhaps a photo, in the local newspaper, and the citizens of the devastated community receive the help they need. These acts of generosity also tend to result in a significant amount of paid-for business following the initial pro-bono work.

In the beginning, you will find that the *local community newspapers are more likely to be interested* than the large daily or national papers. The same applies in the electronic media, since local radio and cable TV stations will probably be more approachable than large national affiliates. Start reading your community papers regularly to get a sense of what kind of stories they generally publish. You have to think like the publisher or editor: what would interest their readers?

Another approach — depending on your type of business — is to offer to write a consumer column at no charge (or in return for a small amount of free advertising). If you have some special expertise that would be of interest to the public, your local paper might be quite happy to take you up on your offer. Newspapers run with very limited resources. They don't have a lot of money to pay writers, and yet they still need a regular supply of fresh, interesting content for their readers. The same arrangement can sometimes be made with local radio stations — especially ones affiliated with a local university or church. If they have segments that bear some relation to your business, offer to be interviewed, to offer some free advice to the public.

Almost every company has unusual things happen to it in the normal course of business, and people like to read about inspiring or funny events. You just have to make an effort to find ways to tell your story in a passionate and exciting way. I recall one situation that hit the papers that could have been a public relations disaster but worked out in the end. We had sent a crew to load a shipment out of an apartment in Edmonton. The customer could not be present, so had arranged for the building superintendent to let us into the apartment and to supervise the loading. Everything went well and the truck was ready to leave for Ottawa when the customer arrived to check on things. That's when it was discovered the superintendent had let us into the wrong apartment. We had a truckload of household possessions belonging to someone who was not moving. Somehow the local press got wind of it and it made the evening news and the local newspaper. Fortunately, the mistake was discovered before the truck left the area. Some might view this as negative publicity because not everyone who heard or read about it realized that we were not responsible for the mistake. But, as they say, "It doesn't matter what they say about you, as long as they spell your name right!"

The topic publicized need not be related to a disaster or a tragedy in order to be newsworthy. One time, a customer's cat got on to one of our moving vans, unbeknownst to our driver, and was transported nearly 2,000 miles across Canada. When the cat was discovered, our local franchisee paid to ship it back to its owners. The story made the papers in British Columbia and Ontario, which gave the company a multiple plug since we had many franchisees in both provinces.

Good public relations are extremely valuable to a company. People view newspaper stories as having more credibility than paid advertisements, so they take notice of your company name and type of business. Whether they realize it or not, this information usually ends up stored in their memory bank, to be brought forth only when they are in need of what you sell. I'd also recommend that you join your local Chamber of Commerce or the Rotary Club. Get involved in your community, do some volunteer work, and make the acquaintance of people in the local media. Naturally, the latter will want to sell you some paid advertising, and in some instances you may want to run a few ads to help keep your company name in the forefront of your community.

If you want to get your name out there without paying a fortune in advertising fees, you have to put as much effort into doing so as you do to selling your product or service directly to a customer. It's not often the media come knocking on your door, so you have to get out there and knock on *their* door. I would encourage any entrepreneur to take time to do some research, to identify whom you should approach, and decide in advance what kind of pitch you are going to use. Employing the services of a professional public relations firm is another option, providing you can afford it.

Another option when paying for ads in print, on the

radio, or on local cable television stations is to *make a contra deal* — you provide your product or service at a highly discounted rate in return for advertising on a similar basis. Many of our offices have used this technique, and since most news organizations have outlets in more than one city, this approach lends itself well to multi-branch or franchise organizations. The key to having success in this area, especially arranging contra deals, is tied to relationship-building. Just as you need to build a relationship with your potential customers (especially corporate clients), you must do the same with media outlets. While it may be possible to phone a newspaper out of the blue to propose a story idea, as I have often done, it will take more work to get them to agree to a contra arrangement for advertising. You must *sell the idea to them based on what they will get out of it* — usually, substantial savings on a product or service they would be in the market for anyway. If you can make a good business case, chances are you may be able to come to a mutually beneficial agreement.

My brother Terry, a master at making contra deals, got the company involved in sports marketing. He initiated the majority of our sponsorship and preferred-mover arrangements with many of Canada's major sports teams. They consisted of contra-type arrangements, whereby sports teams would use our moving services at highly reduced rates in return for exposure in arenas and stadiums, as well as in the teams' promotional and other advertising venues.

Terry was also the brainchild behind the hugely popular "Move of the Game" promotion that we first ran in conjunction with the Calgary Flames, and later with the Toronto Raptors. First, there was a contest for kids to come down to the court to shoot hoops with team members. This was followed by a promotion, where we brought two people from the upper stands down to courtside seats — hence, "the move of the game." In Toronto, the *Toronto Sun* newspaper became involved and provided us with lots of extra exposure. This concept was then expanded to include other sports and other cities. It was a brilliant idea, which made us *stand out from the crowd.*

Another way our moving company stood out was through our association with Canada's Olympic teams. Our direct involvement commenced during the years leading up to the 1984 Olympics in Calgary, when we were on a number of organizing committees. As a result, we got to know all of the right people, including Jim Murray, manager of logistics for the Canadian Olympic Association. It was his responsibility to find suppliers who could handle the teams' transportation and storage requirements. Together, we worked out a sponsorship agreement that saw us provide service in kind in return for being named their "Official Mover." The company received a huge amount of publicity through this arrangement. The cost to us was far less than what other companies paid. You might be wondering how a relatively small company (compared to Coca-Cola or Visa) could make this kind of deal. The answer comes back to *having exceptional people with outstanding relationship-building skills.* It also takes a lot of imagination, hard work, and a good measure of sheer nerve.

Another idea for garnering attention is to find a way to offer *a value-added benefit* to customers when they purchase your product or service. We all know customers like to get a little something extra when they make a purchase. I pride myself on the fact that our moving company was a real pioneer in this area. We were always thinking outside the box, which made us rather unique at the time. Since then, many of our competitors have followed suit, but we had the stage to ourselves for quite a number of years.

For example, ours was the first company within our industry to become a partner in a Frequent Flyer program. At the time, Canadian Airlines was one of our best clients, and my brother Terry and I had an excellent relationship with the management group. We recognized there were some obvious synergies between our two businesses, since most of the customers we moved eventually had to fly to their new location. We approached the airline's director of marketing, Blair Baldwin, about putting a program together that would reward our customers with free Canadian Airlines points. We called it "Move and Fly." We negotiated an attractive purchase price for these points, and then launched a successful value-added program whereby customers earned one point for every dollar spent on the transportation portion of their move. We got the word out to the public through the airline's various communication vehicles and via our own sales force. Customers loved the program, and in many cases it was that point of difference that tipped the sale in our direction, when price and other criteria were identical with a competing van line. As you probably realize, most partners in this type of customer loyalty program are usually huge multinational firms. How, then, did a moving company — admittedly, one with a lot of branches across the country — end up with a very lucrative partnership? Once again, it was driven by *relationships and determination.* When Canadian Airlines was bought out by Air Canada, the program was modified slightly under the Aeroplan banner. Atlas Van Lines then took over the management of the program on behalf of all its agents, and today it is extremely popular with Aeroplan's six million members.

Another idea we had that worked out well, and which was conceived by one of my sons who was a ReMax agent, was our Real Estate Cash Rebate program. Any customer who used our referral service was entitled to a $500 cash rebate for either buying or selling a home. If they used our service for both trans-actions, that meant $1,000 in their pocket. It wasn't hard to convince them that those savings should be directed towards their move, so it really was a win-win situation for us. We also created a Mortgage Program with the Toronto Dominion Bank, which gave people 0.5% off the cost of their mortgage if they entrusted their move to our company.

Over the years, there were quite a number of smaller value-added incentives, including free Swiss Chalet coupons, special rates on hotel stays with Westin Hotels, free Canadian Tire certificates, and various other retail promotions. These marketing programs were well received by our customers and added millions of dollars to our company's bottom line.

Today, my Premiere Executive Suites company has a referral program in place with Royal LePage and its 11,000 sales agents and brokers. Such arrangements are helping us grow at an exponential rate. You always have to be on the lookout for ways to find new chan-nels to promote your business.

It's true that what was once new and unique could

now be considered rather commonplace. Loyalty programs abound; however, this doesn't mean that you, too, can't find unique ways to promote your business using a value-added approach. If your business is a single location, then look for local retailers or other businesses who might want to partner with you to provide customers with that much-appreciated extra. If you are part of a network that has locations across the country, then you should look at national affiliations.

Never discount the value of *creating some excitement* around your value-added offerings. Giving customers more than they expect is part of the recipe, but making them understand the perceived value they've received is also a crucial ingredient in the mix. This means you have to actively promote whatever your offer, each time you make contact with your customers.

If you have a retail type business, hold *open houses or other exclusive events at your place of business* by special invitation. A number of furniture stores, car dealers, and high-end women's clothing stores are doing this. Invite existing customers to a special VIP event where they can purchase your product at a special discount. To make it more attractive, add a little flair to the event with draw prizes, refreshments, and maybe some entertainment. People love to be considered special. Use the term "Preferred Customer" or something similar on your promotional material.

In our moving business, we held customer information nights where we demystified the process of moving, gave demonstrations on packing, and answered questions. The goal was to showcase our capabilities.

Our company's annual "Customer Appreciation" evenings were another way we set ourselves apart from our competitors. We started out in the early days with a small function that included about 20 guests. Eventually, the functions became much larger with 250 to 300 guests. These were quite glamorous affairs with interesting and eclectic entertainment, a gourmet meal, and an open bar. It's true they were very expensive to put on, but the guests represented millions of dollars in business so it was worth it. As the old saying goes, "Business begets business." When you spend time with clients in a social setting, you strengthen the bond between them and your company. This encourages their continued patronage, providing your product or service continues to meet their needs.

As we did in the moving business, we have been doing our best to bring attention to Premiere Executive Suites. We currently have about 500 properties in Canada. Because we are not in the same league as some of the big players in the business, such as Bridgestreet or Oakwood, who have 10,000 and 22,000 properties respectively, we decided to take a different marketing approach. Premiere is being promoted as having unique, boutique-type properties that provide a real home away from home experience. Like other companies in our industry, we exhibit at a variety of conferences. In 2004, we took booth space at the Canadian Employee Relocation Council's conference in Newfoundland. The delegates who attended were representatives of corporations that relocate employees. As such, they were an ideal target audience for the service we sell.

We knew we were not going to be the only company of our type there, so we wanted to be a bit more creative. Instead of setting up a regular display booth, as did all the other suppliers, we used our space to set up a comfortable living room, creating an inviting atmosphere that encouraged people to come by, sit down, and talk to us.

We added an entertainment element with a strolling fiddler and an accordion player. My partners were out in full force to extend some hospitality and to make our guests feel comfortable. They were still able to sell, but in a very low-key manner, which people appreciated. To make things even more fun, we had draws every 15 minutes for the nicest, softest teddy bears imaginable. Few people can resist a teddy bear. We also held a final draw for a mammoth-sized one. This turned out to be one of the best ideas we've ever had. Many of our competitors expressed envy, so I won't be surprised to see lots of living room sets at next year's conference. ("Imitation is the kindest form of flattery" didn't become a cliché without a reason.)

In one value-added experience with Premiere, we decided to go the social route by having an annual picnic on my property out in Chester, Nova Scotia. At first, 50 to 100 people participated, but last year we ended up with over 700 people. To help promote the event, company banners were hung around town during Chester Race Week, which got us a tremendous amount of exposure since this is one of the most prestigious boating events on the eastern seaboard. We ran shuttles from the Chester Yacht Club to bring people out to the oceanfront location, set up barbeques, and hired Lenny Gallant, winner of 13 East Coast Music Awards, to provide entertainment throughout the entire afternoon. Because we created such a festive atmosphere, we were the talk of the town.

Creating buzz for your company can also be

achieved through *network marketing*. Once again, our moving company was well ahead of its time in this area. We were one of the first companies to market our services to the members of various associations. The cost to do this type of marketing, understandably, will vary depending on the association involved. However, when you consider that you are being given the opportunity to sell your product or service to a very targeted audience, the cost usually can be justified.

Some associations want a specific percentage of the sale in the form of a commission or rebate, while others look for a flat dollar amount in annual partnership or sponsorship fees. Advertising in their various communication vehicles is also part of the marketing mix, however you can usually negotiate preferential rates or some form of contra deal. Either way, as long as the group is large enough and has the right demographics, this approach can be a cost effective way to market your services.

The first step is to establish credibility with the association or other organization. You have to *sell them on the idea that you have a product or service that will be of value to their members.* If you can do this successfully, then you have opened a valuable channel for marketing. Naturally, you will only want to work with associations or organizations that have good reputations. Once an association or other group endorses your product or service, their members will be predisposed to consider doing business with your company. They will view your company as one they can trust to deliver on its promises — and in business today, gaining trust is half the battle.

There are literally thousands of associations out

there. Some are local or regional; others are more national in scope. Do a little research, and try to identify a few that you believe would be a good fit with your business. To inspire you, I'll give you some examples of what we did. When AMJ purchased a competitive group of moving companies (CP Moving, owned by Canadian Pacific Enterprises), one of the corporate salespeople we inherited was already dealing with Jacques Rocheleau from the 30,000-member Ontario Medical Association (OMA) on a very successful program. One of the salesperson's co-workers, Elaine Shaw, noticed how many calls came in from prospective customers, and decided that working through an association might be a good way to reach a whole group of potential customers at one time.

Elaine had recently become a member of the Canadian Automobile Association (CAA), and had received her membership kit, which included information about special value-added benefits and savings to members offered by various CAA-endorsed partnerships. After doing some research, we learned that CAA had over three million members (which made it a very attractive target). We contacted their head office in Ottawa, and made an initial presentation. The association expressed some serious interest, and invited us back to present to their board of directors. I became personally involved at that point, and after some protracted negotiations, we were able to put a program together. We generated a lot of business from this partnership.

At first, it was a full-blown national program, managed through CAA's head office. After a few years, however, the organization's regional offices put pressure on the association to allow them to put their own provincial programs together. We modified the program to meet these needs, and it continued bringing in new customers.

With this success under our belt, we turned our sights on the 500,000-member Canadian Association for the Fifty Plus (CARP) who represent an important segment of our society. CARP advocates for seniors and soon-to-be seniors on issues including pension plans, health care benefits, and other areas of interest and concern. For the most part, CARP's members are affluent and often in need of a mover. Who better to market our services to? In April 2005, Lillian Morgenthau and Eric Vengraff of CARP agreed to endorse my new company, Premiere Van Lines, as their preferred mover. We advertised in CARP's publications, promoted preferred rates for their members in our own sales literature, and worked to build a relationship with the organization's management. Once more, we saw huge returns on our investment in terms of new business.

While we had the advantage of a coast-to-coast multi-branch company that would appeal to the larger national associations, you can do something similar on a smaller, local, or regional scale. Service groups, local chapters of professional organizations, local school boards — the list is virtually endless. The same goes for partnering with other local businesses, or becoming a sponsor supplier to your local Welcome Wagon chapter. People like and appreciate special offers, so give some thought as to how you can be a bit more creative. Before you know it, your name will be well known within your community.

KEY LESSONS LEARNED

- Continually think up ways to attract new customers, and how to make your business known
- Stay ahead of the competition by thinking outside the box
- Call your local newspapers and radio stations and tell them what exciting things you are doing. Make them want to report about you and your business!
- A humourous business anecdote or public-service story is usually well received
- Consider contra arrangements in lieu of full paid advertising
- Value-added benefits can add great value — and great profits — to your business
- Look around and see how other companies could make great mini-partners on countless different projects
- Do some event marketing to help create excitement
- Network marketing is often a great way to go

CHAPTER ELEVEN

DON'T PUT ALL YOUR EGGS IN ONE BASKET

"Buy land, it's the one thing they are not making any more of."
— *Author Unknown*

While this book is intended to give entrepreneurs or aspiring entrepreneurs advice about building their business, I wanted to include a chapter on another form of investment: real estate. There are a couple of reasons for this. One is that I believe it's important not to have all of your money tied up in your business. Equity in a business is not as liquid as other forms of investment. If you need money quickly, it's easier to sell a few pieces of real estate than try to find a buyer for part or all of your business. The second reason is that most people become entrepreneurs in order to increase their net worth. Real estate investment is a fairly painless way to do this. In addition, if you get into real estate in a bigger way, such as becoming a partner in development projects, then the investment becomes more like a second business.

Over the years I have made a very good living from my moving and accommodations businesses, but to tell you the truth, a great deal of my personal wealth has come from investing in real estate. Every time I received a dividend or a cash bonus I invested it, either in different businesses or, more often, in real estate. And, my Premiere Executive Suites company isn't just a hospitality business. It is also a real estate investment business. Therefore, I'd like to share some information and anecdotes about my foray into the world of land, bricks, and mortar.

There are many other places to invest money, including side businesses, stocks, bonds, commodity futures, gold bars, and precious gems. I've tried them all, but I'm much more likely to invest in real estate than in the other areas mentioned above. It's been a great love of mine for over 30 years. Real estate has long been considered one of the best places to invest money since it has the potential to increase significantly in value, over time. The equity you build up in this investment is real and will usually be there when you need it. The peace of mind and sense of security you get from knowing you have something to fall back on if times get tough is priceless.

There may also be a deeper, more personal reason why I am drawn to investing in this area. I grew up in a family that was always on the brink, financially. My father was an entrepreneur but not a particularly successful one. To make matters worse, he made a practice of living far beyond his means. This state of affairs made for a very difficult childhood. Outwardly, we were a prosperous family with three homes and luxury automobiles. However, what people didn't realize was that my father put himself in serious debt in order to present this façade. As painful as it is to remember, I can tell you that growing up in a home where we literally had bill collectors at the door was very stressful. This reckless abandon with money created many pressures on my parents' marriage and on our family life. My siblings and I vowed that when we grew up, we would be much more responsible with money. This may be why I choose to invest in property and then make a point of paying off my mortgages as quickly as possible. A psychiatrist would probably say this gives me the sense of security that was so lacking in my childhood.

Emotions aside, it's a known fact that 95% of millionaires in Canada are seriously involved in real estate investment. Why not try what has worked for that select group? Please do not confuse me with that fellow who runs those infomercials from his yacht in the Caribbean, who tells you that *You Can Become a Millionaire Overnight With No Money Down*. Real estate is like any investment, in that you have to be both informed and knowledgeable. Start paying attention to newspaper and magazine articles on real estate; befriend a real estate broker to learn more about their business. You will quickly become attuned to this investment field.

A good working relationship with realtors is worthwhile cultivating. Once a realtor knows you are on the lookout for deals and are in a position to make a quick decision, they will keep you informed about what's going on in their area. Being able to move quickly is the critical component. One realtor that I know, George Edwards from Prudential, specializes in condominiums in the Halifax area. One of the properties he handles is a prestigious building called Charter House. In 2000, he called me to say that he was listing a condo in that building at 9:30 a.m. I knew it was a hot market and the property would sell quickly so I told him I would meet him at 10:00 a.m. At the meeting, I put in an offer at $132,000 against the asking price of $135,000. He presented it to the owners and it was accepted less than an hour after it went on the market. The property is worth about $290,000 in today's market.

My friend Sam Joubran is a committed real estate investor. He explains investing in this sector as follows:

> To consider whether real estate represents a wise option to meet investment expectations, it must be compared to other investment vehicles. The final determination is based on four benefit outcomes:
>
> 1. Reduction of risk to an overall investment portfolio
> 2. Protection against inflation shocks
> 3. Provision of relatively high rates of return
> 4. Reasonably high levels of investment income
>
> As with any investment strategy, diversification of real estate investments is an important consideration and this means investing across property types and geography. There are four basic types: residential, industrial, retail, and office. Real estate can be an excellent alternative to equity holdings, especially when you consider the kind of shocks experienced by the equity markets since 2000. Investment in real estate can help achieve long-term targets and reduce overall risk.

In a nutshell, investing in real estate is a hedge against other forms of investment or downturns in the economy. The stock market has been particularly volatile over the past decade. Many people were seriously hurt when the big tech bubble burst in and around 2000. Many small investors and small business owners nearly had their entire retirement portfolios wiped out because they had gotten on the "tech ride." Since then, financial experts will tell you that a lot of people have returned to other forms of investment, with real estate being one of the primary ones. Canadians are generally fairly conservative investors, which may explain why we view real estate as such an attractive investment. I guess it comes down to the belief that it is a safe place to put our money.

Most of us are aware that real estate has its cycles, and is impacted by a variety of external factors including interest rates and the general state of the economy. Historically, every decade or so we see a significant downturn in the real estate market. But I don't want you to think that you always have to wait for a downturn in the market in order to jump in. You can still invest in real estate when prices are high; you just have to be sure you are getting a good deal. Buying in when the market is starting to soften can be a good time, because sellers are usually a lot more motivated. They know they've missed the peak, and can be concerned that things will only get worse. This is when I tend to be a bit of a scavenger. I'll often offer 20% to 30% below the asking price, and surprisingly I sometimes end up having my offer accepted, with only a few sign-backs.

It might sound a little ghoulish, but I've also had success with estate properties. Often, the heirs of the deceased are in a hurry to sell, and are more amenable to a lower price, just to get rid of the property. You don't need to stoop to reading the obituary pages, but your friends in the real estate business or a local lawyer can make you aware of the circumstances for a sale.

Of course, different sectors are not always affected at the same time. Commercial real estate, especially very large projects, is not the place for the novice investor. You can get into serious trouble if you don't know what you are doing. However, residential real estate, particularly properties that can be rented for a period of time, is usually a safe bet. As a rule, I've found the profit ratio on more modest properties to be greater than on the higher-end ones.

For over three decades, I have preached to anyone who would listen about the value of diversification, especially through real estate investment. The people I talk to about this are often of modest means. Many small business owners don't have a lot of excess cash for other investments. Most of their money gets reinvested in their business to help it grow. This makes sense, but I still think that having some investments not tied to the main business is a good idea. *You don't have to be wealthy to start investing in this area.* I think I gravitated towards real estate because it was a *tangible* investment. I can see — and feel and touch — what I bought. Even when I rented out the property, I could still drive by and look at it, knowing it was mine (and the bank's). It gave me a good feeling. In a way, it's more like making a retail purchase where you leave the store, merchandise in hand. Real estate investment is relatively affordable for people who don't have a huge financial stake. The investment is guaranteed to increase in value at some point. The secret is knowing when to buy and when to sell. The good news is it's not that hard to spot the trends, you just have to pay a little attention to what's going on in the market. And even if you do make some mistakes, they are usually not as costly as picking the wrong stock. For over a century, real estate has maintained its investment appeal with prices escalating on a regular basis in spite of a few bumps along the way.

When I started out in the moving business, I supplemented my income with other businesses, including painting, carpet cleaning, and pong games in bars — the latter being the forerunner of today's video games. I wanted to earn as much money as I could, so I was willing to try anything. But once I had money to play with, I invested part of it in the moving business (usually buying more trucks), and the rest I invested in real estate. In those days, I wasn't dealing in big investments; I came up with the down payment, then found a good tenant who would pay enough rent to carry most of the mortgage and taxes. My first venture into this arena was in 1972, when I bought a townhouse for $15,000, and a week later was offered $16,000. For someone living in a basement apartment that cost $15 a week to rent, a $1,000 profit seemed like a fortune. Yet, I chose to hold on to it for a few years, at which point I sold it for $24,000. This was the beginning of a life-long love of real estate.

Throughout the 1970s, I bought and sold over a dozen properties, each time realizing profits of between $10,000 and $70,000. For me, it was easier to make money from flipping houses than it was in moving people from house to house.

My wife and I have moved eight times in our nearly three decades of marriage, and each time we've made a nice tax-free profit on the sale of our house. Our first house was bought in 1977 on Church St. in Beaconsfield, Quebec. We paid $60,000 for it and sold it two years later for $90,000. The next property was purchased in 1980, a lovely house in Pointe Claire, for $155,000. In early 1981, barely a year later, we decided to move to Toronto, and sold the house for $250,000, thus making $95,000 tax-free profit for our brief stay there. I've made it a practice to buy and sell at least one piece of real estate every year for my personal portfolio. (This is separate from the real estate deals that are part of Premiere Executive Suites.) In 1987, I bought 5.5 acres on the tip of Chester Peninsula, just south of Halifax, for $475,000. I quickly subdivided two lots — a total of 2.75 acres — and sold them for $475,000. This left me with nearly three acres of prime oceanfront property *for free*. This is where we built our dream home, and it's the one property my wife refuses to sell at any price — in spite of some incredible offers received.

There are further real estate lessons to be learned from those two subdivided lots in Chester, to see how real estate can get exceedingly interesting. One of the lots sold for $210,000 in 1988, and I bought it back in 2001 for $225,000 since the owner needed quick cash. One week later, Tim Harris, a local realtor who specializes in properties on the South Shore, called me to report that he had a buyer who would pay $450,000 — twice the price I had just paid. My wife didn't want to sell it at the time — God bless her — so I declined this amazing offer. In 2003, a mere two years later, we sold that lot for $1.1 million! The deal was just too good to pass up *that* time.

In the fall of 2004, I bought a home on a large lot in Chester, where properties have increased tenfold in price in the past few years. Originally, the owners were asking $360,000, but since this is primarily a summer community, the house was still on the market in early September. I offered them $220,000. They countered at $315,000; I counter-offered; and we settled on $235,000. I then subdivided the lot, sold the house for $210,000 within a couple of weeks, and put the second lot up for sale at $150,000. At worse, I'll end up clearing between $90,000 and $100,000 for minimal time and effort.

In January 2005, I was discussing the possibility of developing a new property on the water in St. John's, Newfoundland, with my good friend Bill Mahoney. The project would be a combination of privately owned, high-end condominiums and a number of units for Premiere Executive Suites. Each section of the building would have a private entrance and we would share the amenities and facilities, which would include a fitness club and perhaps a restaurant. This would be an incredibly exciting project that I'm sure will come to fruition. It will be the first of its type in St. John's. I'm delighted to be invited in as a partner, and am pleased that I've earned the right kind of reputation that allows people of Bill's calibre to respect and trust me enough to give me this opportunity.

While I realize that some of the deals I've been involved in — especially the commercial ones — are rather sophisticated, my point should be clear: *I started as a young man with just a single property, a small down payment, and a good tenant.* As I became more successful, I tried to come up with a 25% down payment, which eliminated the extra cost of CMHC mortgage insurance. Then, I made a point of taking the shortest amortization period I could afford, usually 12 to 20 years, so that I could pay down the mortgage more quickly and increase my equity in the property. I've also never been afraid of taking on properties that needed some renovations. It's amazing how much you can save on a property that looks a little run-down, but has the potential to increase in value with a little sprucing up.

Real estate investing is a great way to invest some of your profits from your main business. Here are some key points to consider before buying investment real estate.

1. **Location, location, location.** The realtor's famous mantra is a wise one. When scouting locations, always ask yourself, "Would I live here?" Always buy in an attractive-looking neighbourhood, or buy in an area that is being gentrified.

2. **Watch the cycle.** When prices are high, be careful of overpaying. It's better to wait until the market starts to soften. Vendors are usually more motivated at this time because they are afraid they might miss the opportunity to make a good profit. Look for bargains and always offer considerably less than the asking price (unless it is a really hot market).

3. **If you find an excellent bargain, move quickly, otherwise you may lose out.**

4. **Keep abreast of what is going on in your community to help you spot opportunities.**

5. **How easy is it to get good tenants?** Will their rent cover a good percentage of your expenses?

6. **Do you have a sufficient down payment?** I recommend a minimum of 25%.

7. **Are you prepared to make sacrifices in respect to your time (by being a landlord), and the financial commitment it will take to pay for the property?**

I should warn you that you will feel a little overwhelmed and somewhat scared when you start signing for properties. It's a big responsibility, and a big commitment, but it will pay off in the end.

Today, I personally own 50 properties, and I'm always looking for the next deal. In December 2004, I was looking for a condominium in Toronto. I ended up buying two at Palace Pier, a luxury property on the lake, at a price of $250 per square foot, which is a real bargain in the Toronto market. In contrast, the Intrawest project of condos and time-shares in Collingwood are selling for as high as $700 per square foot. Because I knew the condominium market in Toronto was starting to soften, I was able to negotiate a good deal. And from my decades of experience, I know that when the time comes to sell, I'll make a healthy profit.

Investing in real estate is usually foolproof, but it's also important to remember that the economy moves in cycles and some form of downturn or even a recession is likely to occur every eight to ten years. Just be prepared for it and don't get in over your head. I wish you the same good fortune as I have had in the world of real estate.

KEY LESSONS LEARNED

- Investing in real estate is a great way to increase your net worth
- Educate yourself about the field
- Start with small residential rental properties
- Do what you have to in order to scrape together a 25% down payment
- Shorten the amortization period on your mortgage to increase your equity position

CHAPTER TWELVE

WOMEN IN POWER

"Whatever women do they must do it twice as well as men to be thought half as good. Luckily this is not difficult."
— *Charlotte Whitton*

Throughout this book, I have mentioned a number of women partners who have made major contributions to my personal success and that of companies I have owned or co-owned. I feel blessed to have met and worked with these women, but I am most grateful to be able to count them among some of my closest friends. A few of these relationships go back to my earliest days in business, while others are more recent. I have profound respect and admiration for these women, not only for what they have helped me accomplish, but also for the success they have achieved in their own right.

It might surprise you to learn that women-led companies provide jobs for 1.7 million Canadians, which is a greater number of jobs than those created by Canada's top 100 companies. **Women entrepreneurs are creating jobs at four times the rate of the average firm.** By definition, a woman-led company is one where the woman is president, owner, co-owner, or partner. A landmark study was done for the Bank of Montreal (BMO) in 1998 that uncovered some startling facts about women entrepreneurs, painting a very positive picture from both a social and economic perspective. Here are a few interesting facts:

- There were more than 700,000 women entrepreneurs in Canada
- Women owned or operated 30.3% of all firms in Canada — nearly one third!
- The number of women-led firms is increasing at double the national average of 19.7%
- Women-led firms lead new business growth in every province
- Canada is the world leader in the percentage of women business owners
- Women-led firms are as financially strong as the average firm
- Women-led firms are as tenacious as the average firm, with a 78% survival rate
- Women-led firms are a significant and growing force in Canada

The study also compared women entrepreneurs in Canada to those in the United States, and found that facts were similar in both countries. Overall, the study proved that women have been at the forefront of Canada's transformation into a service-based economy, and the future looks bright for women who want to venture into the world of entrepreneurship.

Catalyst, a research and advisory organization that promotes the advancement of women in business, put together another interesting survey for BMO. Catalyst examined two measures of financial performance: return on equity (ROE), and total return to shareholders (TRS). The study found that *companies with a higher percentage of women in senior management roles* had a 35% higher ROE and a 34% higher TRS. Results like this should go a long way towards eliminating bias against women in the world of business.

Government agencies like Industry Canada are already putting programs in place that are tailored to women. Recently, they co-sponsored a forum that brought together academics, community leaders, politicians, and civil servants to create a blueprint on how best to support women entrepreneurs. Other Crown corporations like the Business Development Bank of Canada set up a special fund to offer financing to women ready to expand their business. Loans from this fund typically start at about $300,000. Women's access to financing has historically been considered a barrier, but current research is proving this may no longer be the case. Banks and other financial institutions are beginning to recognize women entrepreneurs as a very important part of their client base.

The top five sectors where women tend to start businesses are:

1. **Health care services**
2. **Professional or technical services**
3. **Personal or other services**
4. **Retail**
5. **Agriculture**

Other studies have been done since the one initiated

by BMO, and they have all echoed the projections of earlier ones. By 2002, there were 821,000 women entrepreneurs in this country, representing 45% of all small businesses and contributing $18.109 billion annually to the Canadian economy. The trend towards self-employment continues, and women entrepreneurs make up an impressively large share of this group. Perhaps this is one reason why the major banks, accounting firms, and business magazines (such as *Profit*) have all established annual Recognition Awards specifically directed at women entrepreneurs.

An article appeared in the November 15, 2004 issue of the *National Post*, honouring the winners of the 2004 Rotman Canadian Women Entrepreneur of the Year Awards, presented by BMO Financial Group. "This year's winners represent the true spirit of Canadian entrepreneurship, and have successfully forged new paths in a wide range of businesses," declared Michelle Field, BMO's vice-president, commercial market. "Their achievements stand as an example . . . to all entrepreneurs."

I'm pleased to learn that the women I've partnered with over the years mirror the profile of some of the most successful women entrepreneurs in the country. Like many of the winners of these various awards, my female partners are married and have children. They know full well how hard it is to balance family responsibilities with running their business. In effect, they have two jobs.

The women I work with certainly manage this difficult double role and constantly amaze me with their competence. On the job, I see them as dynamic, talented businesswomen able to tackle any challenge, but

I know at the same time they do their utmost to ensure their families' needs are also met. I have no problem admitting that I could not do what they do, and I think most men would agree with me.

I'm also very proud to say that while my partners have yet to win any awards created specifically to honour women entrepreneurs, they have received public recognition for their accomplishments. Premiere Executive Suites was honoured with two Gold Awards from the Chambers of Commerce in Montreal and Halifax. The most recent was the Gold Award for Small Business of the Year, Atlantic Region, sponsored by the *Globe and Mail*. The award was presented at a black-tie gala in Halifax in late January 2005. I can't begin to tell you how proud I was of our group when they ascended to the stage to accept this prestigious award.

Although it was not by design, many of my partners (especially in Premiere Executive Suites) are women. I see this as a positive thing, especially when you reflect on the good news about women entrepreneurs that I've detailed above. Having female partners is not a totally new experience for me. From the beginning of my career, I saw the great value in partnering with women, especially in their ability to develop and nurture relationships with employees and customers.

When I started in the moving business, it was — and still is, to a major degree — a male-dominated industry. In spite of that, I never had any reservations about hiring women in key positions. I have always made it a point to hire the best talent available. It just so happened that many were women. Perhaps it was growing up with a strong mother and three sisters that made me more inclined to accept women as equals. One woman to whom I will always be grateful is Jackie Stewart, who I told you about in an earlier chapter. There's no doubt that I would not be where I am today if it wasn't for her. When she retired, I had a portrait of her hung in the front foyer of our corporate headquarters. It was a small gesture to demonstrate how much she meant to everyone, and to show that her contribution to the company's success was both acknowledged and appreciated. To this day, she remains one of my closest friends. Jackie has recently agreed to join the board of directors for Premiere Van Lines. I know she will make an important contribution to this new venture.

There have been many other women of this ilk over the years who have achieved tremendous success. If I had to explain why, I think I would say the one thing these women all have in common is their incredible talent to build relationships. They treat their customers like friends and family, not just business associates, thus garnering their clients' respect and loyalty.

I'm proud to say that over the years, the companies I've been associated with have had more women managers, partners, and top salespeople than has been the case at any of my competitors. Without exception, they have proved themselves to be every bit as strong and determined to succeed than any man I know.

Women may be more emotional and sensitive than men may be, at times, but this doesn't detract from their abilities; rather, it adds a different dimension to day-to-day operations. I am known to be a fairly emotional person, so perhaps that's why I relate so well to women. And women are more likely to be team players than most men. I've also found women generally have good instincts. I, too, make many of my decisions based on whether something feels right. My partners are all professional in their approach to business, but at the same time they are caring and compassionate human beings. Each has earned her success through hard work, dedication, and total commitment.

In the following section, you will hear directly from a few of the wonderful women with whom I have worked. They will talk about their business, working relationships, friendships, and the joys of being an entrepreneur. They will also share the reasons why they have been successful, what attributes they possess that have allowed them to step into the role of entrepreneur, and what challenges they face.

Tatiana Kredl, President
Premiere Executive Suites, Montreal

Background:
- 40 years old; originally from France; lived in Montreal approximately 14 years
- Studied interior design in France and Boston
- Married to David, an Air Canada pilot; has two daughters, aged 14 and 11
- Father was an entrepreneur, and she always wanted her own business
- Joined Premiere in December 2000. Owns 47.5% of the Montreal company with her husband (but it is she who runs it)

I was a stay-at-home mom for quite a few years. My husband's job takes him away a lot of the time. But even when he's at home, he is quite busy with a side business that he operates, so it was important for me to be there for my girls. At the same time, I will admit there was a part of me that was dissatisfied with my life, and I didn't like feeling that way. Like many women, I wanted something for "me." I had always wanted to have my own business, and while I was good at interior design, I knew it wasn't the business I wanted to devote all my time to; I was just not that passionate about it. I took on a few design projects when the girls got older, which is how I first met Tim. I was doing some work on the new building for his moving company branch in Montreal. To be honest, I knew nothing about him or the moving company, but I was immediately struck by his personality. It's very rare to find a man who is so successful in business, yet also down to earth, caring, and always treating everyone he meets as if they were his equal.

When Tim told me about Premiere, I couldn't wait to be part of it. I think I shocked him with how quickly I agreed to become involved. As soon as he explained the concept, I instinctively knew this was the opportunity I had been waiting for. It just felt right, and I'm a big believer in fate; that the right thing will come along at the right time. His vision and his values matched my own. I've moved a number of times, and I know what it's like to feel displaced, yearning for home. I could see this business blended all the things I'm good at: helping people, creating an inviting environment, working hard, and making a success by doing things *my* way. Now, I don't want you to think it's been easy. Going into business created some waves in my life.

I may be the president, but I'm working at least 60 hours a week, plus I still have to balance that with my family responsibilities. So far, my husband and daughters have been quite understanding, and that's helped. I think of this business as my "third baby." Just as I nurtured my children, I'm doing the same with the business. It's been good for my self-esteem and my confidence. Each little success propelled me forward to the next one. It's great!

I also felt comfortable having Tim as a partner. He's very good at trusting people, and empowering them. At the same time, he's always encouraging you, telling you what a great job you are doing. He really cares about his partners, and that makes you want to excel so you don't disappoint him. The rest of the Premiere group is fabulous as well. We all get along, and have become fast friends. We all love what we do, and we'll go out of our way to help each other. It's like being part of a great family, entertaining clients together and visiting with each other's families. We are even able to disagree without it causing any strain.

Tim's a real visionary and a real dreamer. Sometimes, it's a little scary. For example, when he decided to do a complete restoration on an old B&B in a Montreal suburb, turning it into a first-class inn, I got a little nervous. My husband and I have invested about $300,000 to date, including 20% of the inn property. The restoration alone cost over $2 million, and that's on top of the $500,000 for the property. So, Tim took the majority interest in this particular project. Now that it's finished, he leases back the units to our Montreal company, and

it's my job to make sure we keep them occupied.
This is a prime property, so I need to find clients
who will appreciate it, and be willing to pay a fair
dollar. It's a challenge, but one that I'm up for.

I'm really committed to making a success of this
company. I've discovered I'm really ambitious,
resilient, and gutsy. I like being involved in every
aspect of the business. Whether it's making cold
calls on corporations, attending Chamber of
Commerce functions, dealing with suppliers, choosing or supervising the interior decoration of new
units, or any one of a hundred other things, I feel in
control. I believe that's why I've been successful. I
also think it's good for my daughters to see that
women can be a success in business. That's not to
say everything I've done has worked out. I've made
some mistakes, a couple of them quite serious, but
I've learned from them. Now, we're up to 60 units,
mostly in Dorval and downtown Montreal, and
have about $5 million worth of real estate. Our
sales revenues are around $2 million and profit for
2004 was $200,000. We're ready to expand, prob-
ably with more downtown units. We want to keep
growing. And I'm prepared to do whatever it takes
to make this happen. It's been an exciting few years.
I'm doing what I always wanted to do, and enjoying every single minute of it. I'd recommend
entrepreneurship to anyone.

Judy Sandor, Vice-President, Corporate Sales
Premiere Executive Suites, Montreal

Background:
- Turned 40 in December 2004
- Married to a fireman; has two children, aged 16 and 14
- Was previously in charge of the executive floor at the Dorval Hilton for 18 years
- Joined Premiere in September 2001; owns 5% of Premiere Montreal

Like Tatiana, I'm a big believer in fate. In fact, I met my husband when he was dispatched to the site of a car accident in which I was involved. We exchanged numbers, and the rest is history. We've been married for 18 years. A chance meeting brought me together with Tatiana. She and her husband were meeting with Tim at the Hilton. I just happened to be on duty that evening. We talked, and later Tatiana approached me about joining Premiere. Tim and I have known each other for years, since he was a regular guest at the hotel. He saw how I handled my work, and I guess he and Tatiana decided I had what it took to fit in with their business. I agreed to Tatiana's offer on a trial basis. The business is similar to what I was used to, but the working environment is so much better. At first, we worked out of Tatiana's home, and then we purchased a great historic house that we renovated for use as offices and accommodation units. I'll admit it was a little scary to leave the Hilton, but I just felt in my heart that this opportunity was too good to refuse. I started out as Vice-President,

Guest Services, and then I became Vice-President, Corporate Sales in the latter part of 2004. In November, I made my first big presentation to Royal LePage, and I can tell you I was scared to death, but it went well. Tatiana supported me all the way. Now there are ten of us in the Montreal location, and we have so much fun that it almost doesn't feel like work. I feel more appreciated here than I ever did working for the Hilton. I see incredible future potential for the company, and I want to be part of it.

Suzanne Bachur, Senior Vice-President
Premiere Executive Suites, Halifax

Background:
- 46 years old; moved to Halifax from Toronto in 1980
- Married to Ron, owner of three Swiss Chalet Restaurants; has two children, aged 14 and 12
- Began as receptionist in 1979 at Tim's moving company in Toronto
- Joined Premiere in May 1999; owns 12% of Halifax branch, and has equity position in Montreal, Toronto, and Calgary

From the first day I met Tim, I was impressed. He came across as very smart and very friendly. He was the kind of person you would want to work for, and we became friends. When my husband and I moved to the Maritimes to open a Swiss Chalet restaurant, Tim came in as an investment partner. Over the years, we've done very well in the restaurant business, but when Tim called me in 1999 to ask if I knew anyone he could approach about getting involved with his new venture — what would become Premiere Executive Suites — I offered my services. I was ready for a new challenge. We started out small, with perhaps a half-dozen suites, and now we are up to 145 units.

The years I had spent in the restaurant business taught me a lot about promotional activities, customer relations, and how to motivate staff members. I figured these skills could be transferred to Tim's new business. It was certainly challenging, especially in the beginning. Tim had been busy buying up real estate, but there wasn't any real structure to the company. I took on the task of creating the forms and documents we needed to assist in the selling, leasing, and managing of our real estate. I developed a reservations system, set up schedules for the housekeeping staff, and handled all the accounting so we could keep track of where we were.

Our office employs one part-time and three full-time corporate representatives. In addition, we have an administrative staff of four, a full-time guest services manager, a part-time assistant, a full-time maintenance manager, and six full-time housekeepers. Each year, our staff increases to meet the needs of our growing business. Last year, I developed a new national marketing image that was enhanced by a complete marketing materials package. We have a solidly established brand image and it is really paying off as we expand into other centres across the country.

I really enjoy being an entrepreneur. It gives me a real sense of accomplishment, especially when you see your ideas come to fruition. Having your own business means you can surround yourself with people you really enjoy spending time with. It's challenging and risky, but it's very rewarding. I think I've been successful in part due to all the wonderful people with whom I work. They are enthusiastic, positive, self-motivated individuals, and together we make a good team.

One thing I would tell other women who are considering opening their own business is to make sure you have the support of your family. The hours can be long and it can be a rather stressful way to make a living, so that means your family has to be prepared to make a few sacrifices. If you're always feeling guilty that you're not spending enough time with your family, then you won't be able to give your best to the business. Also make sure you understand what you are undertaking. Talk to other people in the same business to get a better idea of what it is really like. That way you will have more reasonable expectations, and once you have got things up and running you can start to dream big. I guess that is something I learned from Tim.

Tim is a true entrepreneur. He never quits. His drive to expand Premiere into franchises — the same model he used with the moving company — is just wonderful. I have no doubt that we'll have offices right across the country by the end of 2005. I think our success comes from surrounding ourselves with people who love the business, and who are prepared to take service to a totally new level. We'll do anything for our guests, from taking care of their pets to buying their groceries. Whatever they need, we'll supply. Next to my husband, Tim is my best friend. I've learned a lot from him that I apply in life as well as in business. He taught me the importance of always being professional, respectful, cool, and collected, no matter what challenge I'm facing. He's also shown me that focusing on employees' qualities is the way to motivate them and bring out their best. I think I've been successful because I've followed Tim's lead.

Lois Roque, Vice-President, Corporate Sales
Premiere Executive Suites, Toronto

Background:
- 38 years old
- Married with three children (an 8-year-old and 3-year-old twins)
- 15 years prior experience in the accommodation industry
- Joined Premiere in June 2003; owns 45% of Toronto branch with partner Kim Boydell

Like they say, timing is everything. I was working with Bridgestreet, a big player in this business, when I met Kevin Devereaux, who then handled operations for Premiere's Moncton location. He passed my name along to Tim, and when Bridgestreet closed down their west-end Toronto office, I contacted him. Tim put me in touch with Kim Boydell, who was setting up Premiere's Toronto branch, and she and I immediately clicked. It turned out we were born in the same year, both grew up in Brampton — just blocks from each other — and even went to the same high school, but had never met. It's a great partnership, and we are doing well. We started out leasing properties, but now as leases terminate we're looking to buy as many as we can. In 2003, we had a profit of about $10,000 after our first six months in business. The following year, we hit the million-dollar mark in sales, with a projected profit of $120,000. Not bad for a new, young company! I think I'm successful because I understand the business, and I'm willing to pay my dues. I know the dangers of expanding too quickly, and Kim and I are on the same wavelength when it comes to keeping our costs in line. There is tremendous potential for growth here, and I'm really grateful to Tim for allowing us to become equity partners in Premiere. He's willing to share; not everyone wants to do that. However, it makes a huge difference in keeping you motivated if you own a piece of the business.

Kim Boydell, Vice-President, Operations
Premiere Executive Suites, Toronto

Background:
- 38 years old
- Married with two children aged 14 and 9
- Former executive assistant to Tim Moore in the head office of his moving business in Toronto, and former manager of the company's franchise system
- Joined Premiere in June 2003; owns 45% of the Toronto office with partner Lois Roque

Tim's always been a pretty interesting character, and probably one of the most down-to-earth people I've ever met. I think the reason he's successful is that he has great business sense, but an even greater people sense. Working with him for all those years taught me a lot about motivating people. I was ready for a change when he told me he wanted to expand Premiere Executive Suites into the Toronto market. When he started buying condominiums back in 1999, I thought he had lost his mind, but it didn't take long before he had another viable business up and running. Tim's always been a visionary. I should have realized that he knew, at least instinctively, where he was going with this new venture. Already, there are many successful women in the company. I think women are well-suited for business, because we are very good at multi-tasking. We know how to juggle a lot of responsibilities and never let the ball drop. No job is beneath us, as we're willing to do whatever it takes to get the job done. Having Lois as a partner makes it that much easier. We both have the same work ethic, and we are very service-oriented.

I've always thought of Tim as an opportunity maker. He doesn't do anything unless he can make money, but at the same time, he's not greedy. He's willing to share, which is why he offers these partnerships. He could afford just to hire people, but he learned a long time ago that people work harder if they have a vested interest. He also gets as much enjoyment out of his partners' successes as he does his own. He taught me the importance of keeping expenses under control, and that's a great lesson for a new entrepreneur. In fact, maybe he taught me too well, because I continue to work from my home office although Tim keeps encouraging me to find a great house in the Toronto area that I can convert into offices for Premiere.

My family is very supportive of this new venture. I couldn't do it otherwise. My two daughters think it's great that mom has her own business. Even though I still work out of my home they understand that "work time" is different from "home time," and as a result they don't put too many demands on me and are respectful of the time I have to spend running the business. Since we are here whenever our clients need us, it can make for a rather disruptive schedule, but so far the family is coping well. I'm having the best time of my life with this business, and I've discovered there's no magic formula to success. It's a matter of working hard, enjoying what you do, and surrounding yourself with great people.

Diane Jones-Konihowski, President
Premiere Executive Suites, Calgary

Background:
- 54 years old
- Married to former CFL star John Konihowski; has two daughters aged 22 and 16
- Former Olympic pentathlete, Order of Canada recipient, and sports marketing and public relations executive

I've spent most of my life in the sports world. My

husband also works in the sports industry and my daughters are into competitive sports. I felt it was time for a complete change. When the opportunity arose for us to become involved with Premiere, I jumped at the chance. John and I invested some money and I became the hands-on person for our operation. For the first year I operated the business out of our home. My husband volunteered his help when he had time. To be honest, we kind of flew by the seat of our pants in the beginning, learning as we went along. It's hard work, but it's fun. Coming from the not-for-profit world of amateur sport, which is pretty safe, I learned there is a lot more pressure and risk involved in growing a profitable business. The pressure part is keeping our suites full. But I understand pressure having lived it while competing against the best in the world. I'm a very positive person and I like to surround myself with positive people. I have to love what I am doing and believe in the product or service, which I do. I'm not afraid of hard work and I'm a team player, so regardless of what job needs to be done — cleaning a suite or making a bed — I roll up my sleeves and get it done. I think it's important to lead by example. I tell anyone who will listen to find something you love to do and that you are good at — believe in yourself and go for it!

Cheryl Bottomley, Vice-President, Marketing
Premiere Van Lines, Calgary

Background:
- 37 years old
- Married with one child (born in early 2005)
- Former corporate representative at AMJ Campbell with million-dollar sales
- Joined our new moving company in October 2003; owns 10%

I spent six years as a corporate account manager at the moving company founded by Tim. Before I worked in the moving business, I was their client, so I saw first hand how service-oriented Tim and his brother Terry were. When I joined the moving company, I emulated their style, and it certainly worked with my clients. My sales were in the top 5% out of the 150 companies in the system. At AMJ, I worked with Terry Moore, but left after he was terminated, due to political issues with the new management of the company. I went to work for the Pattison Group, but I knew that I wanted to work with Terry again if an opportunity arose. When his non-compete clause expired, I called him and said I'd be interested in joining his new company. But I made it clear that I wanted to be an equity partner, which is what I became in the fall of 2003. Moving from paid employee to entrepreneur has been both scary and amazing. I took a risk, but I think it was a well-calculated one. Tim understands, whether consciously or subconsciously, that women tend to be more team-oriented, and I think that's why he gives them opportunities that might not otherwise come their way. He knows that women tend to check their egos at the door, and that they are just there to get the job done. That's the way I work, and so far I've been very successful at whatever I've tried. I'm particularly excited about the future, now that I'm a partner in the new moving company.

Jessica Brown, Senior Sales Executive
Premiere Van Lines, Halifax

Background:
- 45 years old; single
- Highest producing female moving representative in Atlantic Canada

I first met Tim through a mutual friend, and I invited him out to sail with an all-women crew. At that time, Tim wasn't much of a sailor, so here I was, the captain of the boat, barking orders at him! A year later, I was working for him. Before I went into the moving business, I worked for a property management company. Tim had just recently hired a friend of mine, Clint Giffin, and I guess they decided I'd be a good addition to the team. I was rather curious as to how I'd fit into the moving industry, so I agreed to have coffee with Tim. He was so passionate about the business, it was hard not to get excited about the opportunity. He told me about other women who had been very successful in the business, so I decided to try it. Fortunately, I've been quite successful at it. I think women bring sensitivity to the moving experience, because it's much more than just moving furniture. Clients are often stressed, and they really appreciate it when someone takes the time to talk to them and cares about what they are going through. I've learned a lot from Tim that I've put into practice in my job. He's really passionate about his businesses, and that's infectious.

Lyn Leal, Former Owner
Moore Moving, Calgary

Background:

- 40 years old; has two children aged 19 and 7
- Former top producing office moving salesperson at AMJ
- Opened her own moving company in July 2002

I view Tim Moore as my mentor. He is the one who convinced me I had what it took to become an entrepreneur, and run my own moving company. In 2002, I had been the top producing commercial office moving salesperson at AMJ, but I was getting frustrated about not being able to move up the corporate ladder in the Calgary office. It was a bit of an old boys club. One day, I decided to take the plunge, and in honour of my mentor I chose to call my company Moore Moving. It was a good name in the industry, and it worked well for marketing purposes. I'm not sure that he expected me to go one step further and trademark the name, but I did.

(This was a smart move.) I had been quite successful in a relatively short time. I think one reason
women do well in business is that we can play both
sides. I can be the soft woman when it's called for,
but I can also be as tough as the boys when necessary. Women also tend to be more detail-oriented
and more nurturing, which is a plus. We treat our
employees differently, and therefore they go that
extra mile for us. I didn't consider myself the boss;
rather, I was the coach of my team. We also had an
employee profit-sharing plan, which was a good
motivator. With clients, I provided a level of personal service they wouldn't normally expect to
receive from the owner of the company.

I got involved in every aspect of my business,
including the physical packing and moving. The
company grew, and I had 12 full-time employees
and had to buy more equipment. However, I understood that it can be dangerous to expand too
quickly, so I kept a tight rein on expenses. If I had
to identify a couple of things that Tim has taught
me, they would be that you can't do it all alone —
you have to find good people — and the importance of building long-term relationships. You do
that by being honest and ethical at all times. There
are a lot of successful women around, because Tim
either gave them opportunities, or encouraged them
to create their own.

Rosemarie Schoutsen, Account Executive
AMJ Campbell Van Lines, Toronto

Background:

- 48 years old
- Married with 13-year-old twins
- Began as a commercial office representative in 1989; became one of the most successful woman in the field

My role hasn't really changed that much over the years; essentially, it's my job to develop new business for the company. In the commercial office-moving world, this means knowing what's happening, and who is involved in the projects. I'm the one who gets us in the door, and then my team member is the one who goes in to price and try to sell the job. Many of my clients have been with me for years, which I suppose is a mark of success. They've all become my friends. Having strong relationships is key to being a success in business. I think women are good at this, because we bring a more human touch to certain business roles. We remember people's birthdays, we buy little gifts, and these things make people feel good. I enjoyed working with Tim, who was always a big supporter of women. He saw us as equals, and was thrilled when we succeeded.

Some of the women profiled are now millionaires, or well on their way to becoming part of that elite group. In my previous book, *On the Move*, we profiled men who had achieved that degree of net worth. As you can see, there is a common thread that runs through each woman's narrative: hard work, sacrifice, belief in your-self, and willingness to take some risk. If you can do these things, you can achieve both personal and finan-cial success.

KEY LESSONS LEARNED

- Women entrepreneurs are becoming a driving force in Canada's economy
- Women-led companies are as successful as those run by men, and often more so
- Women's relationship-building skills help them to be successful
- Women create nurturing and motivating work environments for employees
- Women are often as ambitious as men
- Women can be successful and still maintain a normal family life

CHAPTER THIRTEEN

LESSONS LEARNED THE HARD WAY

"The way out of trouble is never as simple as the way in."
— *Edgar Watson Howe*

As a lifelong entrepreneur, I have been involved in a number of investments, businesses, and projects. In most cases there have been positive outcomes to these ventures, but there have also been a few situations that got out of control for a variety of reasons. In this chapter I am going to recount three situations that have cost me dearly, either monetarily or emotionally. I've learned a few lessons from each experience that will stay with me for the rest of my life. I'd like to share each of these stories with you to demonstrate that trouble will usually come knocking at everyone's door, but with the right attitude you can survive just about anything. Things can, and do, go wrong on occasion but you just have to remember that business is not brain surgery . . . no one is going to die if things go wrong.

For the most part, I have tried to limit my participation in projects I felt were synergistic to my core businesses. I also don't care for projects where I don't have hands-on involvement. Like most entrepreneurs, I like to be in control. I also like clean, easy deals that you can get into and out of at will. I have, however, deviated from this rule a few times, usually with less than satisfactory results. One such project involved investing in a chain of nursing homes, and to put it bluntly, it was a total disaster.

When a close friend who was a partner at Peat Marwick approached me in 1994 with the idea of investing in a chain of nursing homes, it sounded like a good deal. At the time, we were talking about a fairly small investment, in the range of 5%. My friend had already done extensive research and was convinced it would be the opportunity of a lifetime. To add to my comfort level, he told me that another chartered accountant had agreed to leave his job at Peat Marwick to run the operation. Before we finalized my involvement, I left on vacation. While I was away, tragedy struck. My friend died suddenly. I was devastated at the loss of such a good friend, so when his business partner approached me at a later date about the nursing home deal, I felt I owed it to my friend to be involved in a more major way. You might say that I let my heart rule my head. Although I was originally planning to be a 5% partner, after my friend's death I agreed to take a majority stake in the deal. I even convinced my two brothers, Ted and Terry, to become investors. I guess I felt that I was carrying on my friend's legacy since he had really believed in this project. That was my first mistake.

The nursing home project was the most complex deal I had ever been involved in and meant putting up $2 million in personal guarantees to cover the $10 million in liabilities on the real estate. From the outset, it was apparent this was a difficult and complex business. Our operating partner was a brilliant accountant but he had never actually run a business before, never mind such a difficult one. The number of issues he had to face included labour and operational issues and non-stop challenges with government bureaucrats. To make matters worse, our revenue projections went out the window when the NDP won the election in Ontario and froze the rates paid to nursing homes.

At the time, government-operated nursing homes got approximately 30% more per day per patient than did the private homes. Obviously this was unfair, so the nursing home association we belonged to decided to sue the government. This meant that every member of the association had to pick up a share of the very substantial legal bills. Costs were soaring and revenues were down. This wasn't an auspicious start for a new business.

We had 500 beds in eight centres throughout Ontario. Each day I discovered another reason why I should have passed on the deal. Somehow, the operating partner had neglected to tell me there were unions involved. If there's anything I abhor it's unions. I fought hard to keep them out of the moving business and suddenly I was involved in a business where they were already entrenched. I've always been a believer in treating staff well and rewarding them for good work, but I resent having some union official tell me how to run my business. I figured things couldn't get any worse, but naturally, they did.

The value of our highly leveraged real estate plummeted as Canada struggled through a long and deep recession. Our credit line at the bank went up to $1.1 million and the financial institution wanted another $300,000 in guarantees. Since I was the only one with access to more money, I took on the extra guarantees. In spite of my significant financial contribution, I wasn't involved in any of the day-to-day operations, but I certainly knew the losses were piling up at an alarming rate. One day the operating partner told me he was burned out and had to take a year off. He planned to turn things over to another partner. This was one piece of bad news too many, so I said I wanted out of the deal and told him to find me a buyer.

The company was on the verge of bankruptcy, so it was sold for one dollar. But the sale didn't let us off the hook for all of our guarantees. The bank demanded we pay off the outstanding balance on our line of credit that totalled $1,806,313.34, for which we had put up our personal guarantees. They gave us 24 hours to come up with the money, which I felt was somewhat unprofessional. I was definitely not in a good mood when I went to meet with the bank. It was then that I found out the new operating partner had already had some prior conversations with the bank. As far as the bank was concerned, the company had been given a chance to sort things out. When this didn't happen, the bank issued the 24-hour demand note that had upset me so badly. I was very angry at everyone. Given my level of guarantees I felt I should have been kept in the loop and was distressed at what was happening.

The money owing on the credit line was just part of our obligations. We also owed another $1.3 million to a trust company on the real estate. With liabilities of $3.3 million hanging over our heads, I then learned that the majority partner was virtually bankrupt. Therefore, it was going to be my responsibility to get this thing settled. This is when I went in to survival mode.

Through tough negotiating I settled with the trust company for $625,000, far less than what they could have gone after me for, and made another deal with the bank for $325,000. Those deals still ended up costing me nearly $1 million.

I was angry at the bank for not bringing me into the picture until things were at the point of no return, but I was more angry at myself for getting involved in this complex deal without keeping a closer eye on what was happening on a day-to-day basis. With this much money involved, I should have taken the time to identify where the losses were coming from and to see if I could find some solutions. I also shouldn't have accepted my partner's assurances that things were going to work out. It was a very expensive lesson and one I will never forget. What can you learn from my mistake? First, never invest large amounts of money in a business you know nothing about. Second, don't go ahead with an investment that doesn't feel right just because you feel an obligation to a friend.

My next mistake resulted in a relatively minor monetary loss, but what makes it noteworthy is the fact that it's really about the loss of something that touched me more on an emotional level than on a business level.

In 2000, my friends Larry Smith and Peter Green convinced me that my life wouldn't be complete if I didn't take time to visit the Crane Resort on the island of Barbados. The resort was starting to sell time-share condos, which my friends thought might be of interest to me. The Crane is one of the top ranked resorts in all of the world, so buying a few of these condos would be a smart investment. I also felt it would be great to have a Caribbean location for Premiere Executive Suites.

This would add a whole new dimension to our accommodations business.

When my wife and I first arrived on the island, it was love at first sight. I couldn't imagine anyone not wanting to vacation in this piece of paradise. At the end of our two-week stay, we purchased one of the time-share condos for approximately $80,000 (CAD). At this point, it was a personal investment.

Two years later I returned to the island — this time with my brother Terry. We were captivated by the beauty of the island and its wonderful people. But we were less than impressed with the service we were receiving from the Crane. As someone who knows something about the hospitality industry, I felt their business was ripe for a little competition.

One day we came across a small low-rise facility called Sunrise Beach Apartments. It consisted of a duplex and three small houses. The property was adjacent to the $25-million estate owned by Eugene Melnyk, the billionaire owner of Biovail Pharmaceuticals and the Ottawa Senators. A woman in her late seventies named Lurline came out to talk with us, and one thing led to another and we asked if she was interested in selling her property. She told us people who were interested in buying her property had approached her many times over the years but she really didn't want to sell to them. That's when I suggested that if she sold it to me, I would let her live there rent-free for the rest of her life. She said she would seriously consider my offer.

I realized that to develop the property into the kind of time-share I had in mind would probably mean tearing the houses down. We went back and forth for more than two years and then Lurline told me she had changed her mind, she didn't want to sell. I was devastated. I had already spoken to some people, had partners lined up, and had a good idea in mind of what I would do with the property once I owned it. I was very disappointed but I didn't give up trying. Eventually Lurline agreed to sell and we bought the complex for $700,000 U.S. in March 2003. I was thrilled, and was sure we were on our way to creating a landmark property.

Lurline told me her neighbour John Lashley might be interested in selling his adjoining property. It was about half the size of her lot with a house on it, but trees obscured the view. Still, I figured it might come in handy at some point. Mr. Lashley wanted $500,000 so I offered him $450,000, which he accepted along with my deposit. Things were starting to come together.

I should have known it was too good to last. When I returned a month later, Mr. Lashley told me he had changed his mind and didn't want to sell. Apparently, Eugene Melnyk got wind of my plans to develop the two properties and he wanted to stop me in my tracks. He had applied pressure on Mr. Lashley. What I didn't know was that Melnyk had been quietly buying up most of the surrounding property so that he could keep things exactly as he and his family wanted. I had just gotten a couple of steps ahead of him with these two lots. So being the "hit the problem head on" type of person that I am, I decided to pay Mr. Melnyk a visit. But first I figured I better go see Lurline to find out if she was being pressured too. She told me Mr. Melnyk had offered both her and her neighbour an extra $50,000 each if they could get out of their deal with me.

When I met with Melnyk, he offered to buy the

properties off me and return the money I had already paid out. Frankly, I had no interest in selling but I told him I would take his offer under advisement. To complicate matters a little, Dr. Trevor Carmichael, one of the most renowned and respected lawyers on the island, had been working with me and had planned on becoming a partner in my resort. He had also done some work for Mr. Melnyk and was concerned about retaliation from him. There was a lot of back and forth communication between Melnyk and myself, not all of it pleasant. In the end I agreed to assign the right to purchase the Lashley property to Melnyk for $100,000 U.S., which wasn't a bad return given that I had only put down a $7,500 deposit.

One battle was done, but neither Melnyk nor the owner of the Crane resort, Paul Doyle, wanted me doing anything with the other property. They did everything in their power to prevent me from proceeding with my plans for development.

For example, they tore down a wall between my property and the Crane Resort. Our property had a dead end road that had not been used for over a decade, but suddenly Doyle decided to open the wall up and put in a gate so vehicles could come and go. He did this after I had already ripped up part of the road and begun to landscape. This was followed by an attempt to intimidate my personnel who were supervising my project. No sooner had I returned to Canada than one of my partners, John Scherer, and our property manager, Mauvra Moseley, called in a panic, saying that Doyle had sent a construction crew of 35 men on to our site. They ripped up the landscaping and began to lay cement to recreate the road. I told John (who is a kind and mild-mannered man) to put our Land Rover up against the gate. He did as I asked, but then he called me to say that the construction crew from the Crane were cementing around the car. Both John and Mauvra were feeling threatened by these tactics. I couldn't believe this was happening — it was like a bad movie. I told them to remove the car because I didn't want anyone getting hurt.

The saga continued, problem after problem after problem. I learned that Melnyk was also suing Doyle for building a restaurant at the edge of a cliff. When I was in negotiations with Melnyk over the Lashley property, he had told me there was a geological fracture that went through the Crane Resort property, along my property, and past his own lot. He said a study indicated that the Crane restaurant would fall into the ocean within two years. I wasn't sure if I believed him or not so I told him to get me a copy of the survey. Time went by and the survey never appeared. For all I know it may not even exist. I think Melnyk was just doing a little fear mongering in order to get me to give up on developing Lurline's property.

When bully tactics didn't work, Doyle and Melnyck turned to legal ones. A letter came from the Town Planning department telling us to tear down our gate because we had not received permission to erect it. Interestingly enough, neither Doyle nor Melnyk had needed permission to build their respective gates. That's when I learned an interesting lesson about what one has to do in order to avoid problems when developing property on the island. It's called making a voluntary contribution. Not a bribe of course — just a friendly "contribution." Since this was the first property development project I had ever attempted outside Canada, it came as a surprise to me. However, from what I hear from other businesspeople, this is standard practice outside North America.

It was beginning to look like my plans were being thwarted at every turn, and while I'm not a quitter, I *am* a pragmatic businessman. In October 2004, I called Eugene Melnyk's legal counsel and arranged to have a meeting at Biovail's Mississauga head office. The lawyer was pleasant and professional, but he told me Mr. Melnyk was a billionaire and was also his best friend. Then he drew a circle on a piece of paper and explained to me it represented Eugene Melnyk's sandbox and said I was in it, where I didn't belong. It was an interesting analogy.

I decided that it made sense to negotiate to get the best deal I could. By the end of the day, we had a deal that I was prepared to live with. I came out of the situation with only a small financial loss and I learned that those with power usually get their way. In spite of the farcical nature of some of the antics, I still consider the whole thing to have been a wonderful experience, albeit a frustrating one.

What was *not* a wonderful experience was my most serious business mistake, and my one real regret. Like many entrepreneurs, I failed miserably at succession planning. Intellectually, I knew this was something that should be done well in advance of leaving. In fact, I've always told our managers and franchise owners they should start grooming their successor several years before they plan to step aside. I tell them it's important that they choose someone who can be trusted to carry on the traditions that made their companies successful.

So why, with all of this wisdom, did I fail to take my own advice?

In my opinion, there are two types of entrepreneurs. The first is the type of person who wants to own and run their own business and is happy dealing with the myriad of details and tasks that present themselves on a daily basis. This person is usually perfectly happy doing the same thing until they are ready to forsake the working world and retire to their dream location. Along the way, they may have built up their business into a relatively large entity, or they may have been satisfied to make a good living from their small but flourishing business. Usually, they sell the business and never look back.

The second type of entrepreneur is like me. They thrive on the challenge of creating something more than a business — it's not just about selling products or services and making a profit. Instead, it is a living, breathing entity like a child. As they do with their children, entrepreneurs in this second category put their heart and soul into nurturing their business. This also means nurturing and motivating their employees, and caring in a visceral way for their clients' well-being. These people have become friends and family over the years, and the bond with them continues even if the entrepreneurs are no longer physically present in the office. Because they feel this way about the company they created, it's hard to totally let it go, even when they initiate the transition. Instead of just enjoying themselves or turning to other pursuits, they remain tethered to the company emotionally. While they understand that a new CEO is anxious to put their stamp on the company after taking over, the entrepreneurs find it impossible to turn a blind eye when they see someone hurting the company, especially those employees and partners who helped build it. As irrational as some people may find it, people like me find it necessary to go to any lengths to make that individual understand the harm that will come from their actions. And that is exactly what happened with me.

Before I explain what transpired, I should remind you that I had semi-retired from AMJ back in 1989 after we had sold 70% of the firm to a venture capital group. My partner, Larry Papernick, took over as president and I became chairman. I started spending more time in the Maritimes. But I was called back into full-time service by our investment partner in 1991 when the company got into serious financial trouble. I was reinstated as president and CEO, and a new chairman, Arthur Walker, was appointed. By 1992, the company was back on solid financial footing. It was also the year that Larry decided to resign from the company.

When Arthur Walker joined the company in 1991, I felt like I finally had my own mentor. He was 14 years older than me and had been involved with a number of public companies. He was considered to be a specialist in the area of mergers and acquisitions. It was his idea to take the company public. Our parent company was anxious to take advantage of tax losses they had accrued from the failed A&A Records venture, and Arthur felt that our stock would appreciate in value. Arthur handled the transition from private to public, and I ended up with 650,000 remaining shares. At one point the stock went over $8 per share. Things were good again, so I was anxious to return to the East Coast. I felt I had done my part by helping turn things around. This isn't what Arthur wanted to hear. In fact, he wanted me to take on more responsibility, but I just wasn't amenable to the idea. That brought us to the nub of the matter — who would succeed me as president?

I really hadn't given it much thought, which was poor planning on my part. I had made an effort to interest my brother Terry to consider taking over. He had the skills to handle the job. As well, he was highly respected by everyone in our group. Unfortunately, he and his family had absolutely no interest in coming to Toronto. They had made a great life for themselves in Alberta and didn't want to leave. There really wasn't anyone else in the wings at that point and I suppose I should have waited until I had someone groomed and ready to take over, but frankly, I just didn't want to put my life on hold any longer. I knew Arthur wasn't happy with me in this regard.

In the back of my mind I thought there was one person who was a possibility, but I was also sure that he was far from ready to take over as president. Since I was so anxious to reduce my day-to-day involvement, I figured I might be able to find a way to oversee his development without having to be on-hand on a full-time basis.

The person I was thinking about had been hired in 1992 and became an equity partner. I felt he had potential but that he needed to mature as an entrepreneur. This individual, a former banker from Halifax, was brought in by myself to take over our office installation division. Once he had his foot in the door he approached us about combining its operation with that of our much larger commercial office moving division. I agreed that it made sense. This fellow was bright and ambitious and I knew he could be tough, which was something I figured this division could use.

One thing led to another and eventually I let him take on responsibility for the household goods division; again he did a good job, in terms of financial results. I was there to oversee him and give him advice. I believe I did my best to be constructive in my criticism and viewed it as my mentoring of a possible successor. I should have seen what was to come but I guess I am too trusting and a bit naïve. Behind the scenes, this person did his best to become close to the chairman. I was out of town a fair bit, and during that time he was going around me to get in the chairman's good graces. Before I knew it, they were best buddies, which was fine with me.

Because I had always had a close relationship with my employees, it was only natural that they expressed their concerns to me. I prided myself on our corporate culture. It had taken years to develop it and I felt it was one of the things that set us apart from our competitors. I was beginning to fear that if the culture changed, the company would change — and not necessarily for the better. I have always contended that happy employees make a company more productive and profitable.

From the beginning, it was apparent that my potential successor's management style was very different from my own and our people were having a hard time adjusting. Still, I wanted it to work because I wanted to leave, so I did my best to give him advice. Unfor-tunately, he was not all that receptive to my counsel and this caused some problems between us. I am a fairly laid-back type of executive who tries not to micro-manage my employees. I set expectations for them but then I let them do their job. I know that conflicts arise in any workplace, but I've always done my best to remain calm, even in difficult circumstances. My potential successor, on the other hand, had a rather volatile temper, which he displayed towards me on numerous occasions. I felt he was starting to take too many liberties and that he showed a marked lack of respect for my position as president and CEO of the company. These, combined with his angry outbursts, were giving me reason to doubt his ability to become my successor.

I was becoming really concerned about his inability to control his temper. I felt it was a serious flaw. I've always believed that the CEO of any company must have phenomenal people skills in order to succeed, and must be able to stay calm in the face of conflict. Just being smart and tough isn't enough. But I was running out of options, since there were no other prospects on the horizon. My brother Terry had already declined the opportunity and I knew that unless I wanted to work full-time, the chairman of our parent company would most likely take the decision out of my hands.

By 1999, I had to make a decision. Arthur wanted me back working full time but my wife refused to return to Toronto. I felt the amount of pressure being exerted on me was unfair. After all, I had made a lot of sacrifices for the company over the years. That's when I dropped the ball. I was tired of dealing with this conflict and wanted out so I negotiated a five-year package to be advisory chairman. I still had my doubts about the man who was likely to be my successor, but I tried to push them into the back of my mind. I told myself it would get better and people would adjust to his style. I think in my heart I knew these were false assurances.

My position as advisory chairman was a titular role, but it was understood that I would be an ambassador for the company and I would make myself available to advise and assist the new president. I was prepared to do whatever was asked of me. From my understanding of my self-appointed role, I would spend time motivating franchisees, liaising with major clients, and representing the company at Atlas Van Lines' conventions and other such events. In effect, I would do my best to promote the company wherever and whenever I had the opportunity. From the moment I made this transition, it was readily apparent that I was the last person my successor wanted around. Six months later, he was promoted to CEO.

My relationship with my successor and our chairman had deteriorated dramatically by this point. Because I found it impossible to turn my back on our people, I continued to voice my concerns about how things were being handled. When it was evident that we could no longer talk, I resorted to putting my concerns in writing, which angered my successor. I eventually wrote a severe and very detailed letter criticizing management. I knew when I wrote the letter I was jeopardizing my position and the $175,000 plus expenses compensation that I had negotiated, but honestly, it was a matter of principle. I wasn't prepared to keep quiet just to remain on the payroll. I truly believed the company was being mismanaged.

Things definitely did not improve. I was terminated from my position as advisory chairman. Other terminations followed. Legal actions ensued and numerous resignations were tendered. Then 17 franchisees decided to leave in April 2005 to form their own moving company cooperative. By this time, I was more sad than angry.

I finally came to accept the fact that I had to move

on and leave my feelings for the company I had founded behind in my memory bank. It was now in someone else's hands, for better or worse. Leaving the company is one thing, but leaving the people is quite another. This may partly explain why I have agreed to join a number of my former partners and colleagues in another moving company venture — Premiere Van Lines. You can imagine how much I am enjoying this latest chapter in my business career.

As you can see from my saga, succession planning is something every entrepreneur should take seriously. It is your solemn duty to choose a successor who shares your values and beliefs. Only by doing so can you leave knowing in your heart that you have done right by the company you built.

KEY LESSONS LEARNED

Nursing Home Project
- Be careful about getting involved in businesses that you know nothing about
- Never let emotion get in the way of making business decisions
- Keep a close eye on how things are going with "hands-off" type investments

Barbados Resort Project
- It is difficult to do a development project in another country unless you can be present for an extended period of time to oversee it
- Business styles vary dramatically outside of North America, especially in the Caribbean. They don't have the

same sense of urgency. Government officials are hard to deal with and have their own agenda and priorities

- Before you buy property, know who your neighbours are

Succession Planning

- Succession planning is your responsibility
- Start early to groom your successor
- Don't try to leave or reduce your involvement until a successor is in place
- Once you leave, try to detach yourself emotionally from the company

CHAPTER FOURTEEN

DID YOU FIND JOY?

"Yesterday is history, tomorrow is a mystery, today is a gift."
— *Eleanor Roosevelt*

Life Balance

Ancient Egyptians believed they would be asked two questions upon death, and their answers would determine whether they could continue into the afterlife. The first question was, "Did you bring joy?" The second was, "Did you find joy?" When I read this, I could immediately relate to it since it describes the way I live my life each day.

By now, you know that I believe in hard work, but what you may not yet realize is that I am not a workaholic. There is a crucial difference between the two. It's true that in my earliest, renegade days at TC Moore Transport I worked non-stop and basically did not have a life. However, I was very young at the time, in desperate need of every dollar I could earn. At that point, I didn't have much choice. However, that period is an aberration to the way I've lived throughout the balance of my career.

Happy Personal Life

Having balance in one's life is one of the most difficult goals to achieve on a consistent basis. To reach this nirvana is a journey, and at times a battle, but the rewards are worth the effort. I'd be lying to you if I said it's easy to achieve this, but you must prevail and make it a priority because I genuinely believe you can't be truly successful in business unless you have a happy personal life. The quality of your life outside of work is what makes it possible to tolerate all the challenges, problems, and disappointments that are sure to come at you in your business life. I know that I am truly blessed because of the presence of my wife, Bernardine, and my sons in my life. If I lost everything I own tomorrow, I would still be a rich man because I have their unconditional love and support.

However, I will readily admit that I am a driven and very ambitious man, always have been, and probably will be to the day I die. This is not always easy on my family. There have been many times that my wife has had to rein me in by pointing out to me what's really important in life. Your personal relationship with your spouse and family is the foundation upon whatever other success you may achieve is built. The respect, communication, involvement, and friendship of your spouse are critical. For 28 years my wife has supported me, encouraged me, and motivated me to achieve far more than I ever thought I could. Remember, I was the least likely person expected to succeed. There were many times in my life when my outward show of confidence was simply bravado hiding my inner insecurities. Having someone believe in me the way Bernardine does has made all things possible.

Bernardine has moderated my harshness towards my children, which would sometimes arise in me as it did in my father. She made sure I was properly dressed so I would not look out of place, especially in my early days when I had no fashion sense. Through her kind and loving nature, she softened my view towards others in order that I not be too judgemental. She also accepted my wacky side, with its tendency towards flamboyancy, even if it meant not saying anything critical when I would wear a Harry Rosen suit accessorized with white cowboy boots. She smilingly waved goodbye when I decided to buy a Harley Davidson motorcycle and set off on a long trip across Newfoundland proudly wearing a full set of leathers, although the idea of a possible accident scared her to death. She willingly packed my suitcase for each of my 13 trips to Aspen and Vail with my buddies, even while she was rolling her eyes.

I'm sure she never envisioned herself spending her married life with a man so different in nature, yet she accepts me as I am. Her patience, tolerance, and understanding created a foundation upon which I was able to achieve a degree of success that wouldn't have been possible without her support.

Work Ethic

There was a time when self-confessed workaholics believed that by admitting to this lifestyle they were displaying a badge of honour. Nothing could be further from the truth. Workaholics are usually that way either because they lack confidence in their abilities or because they lack any semblance of a real life. If they have families, they might as well be non-existent for the amount of attention paid to them. Workaholics also ignore their physical health and in many cases abuse it. Workaholics are often dependent on alcohol, drugs, and/or cigarettes. In more recent years, I came to know a number of workaholics. One, who is now deceased, was a senior partner at one of Canada's largest law firms. I always knew that all he did was work, but I didn't realize how bad things were until the time we travelled together and shared a suite. I got up around 3:15 a.m. to use the bathroom and saw a light on in his room. I didn't think much of it at the time, but over breakfast I mentioned it and that was when he told me that 3 a.m. was his normal rising time. The man slept for less than four hours per night.

In my opinion, being a workaholic is not the way to go through life. We are on this earth for such a short time, why would you want to waste it? If I should die tomorrow, no one will remark, "Poor Tim Moore, if only he had enjoyed more of what life had to offer."

Fun and Adventure

I believe in the power of vacations and adventures to dispel some of the pressures that come from working, and many experts agree. Brooks B. Gump, associate professor of psychology at the State University of New York, co-authored a study that examined the vacation habits of men at high risk for coronary disease over a nine-year period. He concluded that the frequency of an annual vacation lowered the risk of death. "What is critical is being able to take true breaks from life's stressors, and, more importantly, taking breaks from potential stress," Gump noted.

Having a sense of fun and adventure goes a long way to helping you de-stress. Spend time playing a sport you enjoy, or take up a hobby. Even try something daring that you never usually would do — like sky diving! The point is to find time for yourself in your busy schedule. It will do you a world of good.

I am a high-energy person who lives for fun and adventure. The high I get from recreational activities rejuvenates me so that I can always be at the top of my game in business. As well, I always have something interesting to chat about with clients and business associates. Life is short. Make the most of your time on this earth.

Balance and Happiness

Fortunately, more people are coming to the realization that you must have some balance in your life. An article in the *Globe and Mail* discussed the results of a survey done with lawyers, a well-known workaholic group. One somewhat surprising result was that there is a new generation of lawyers who list salary well down on the scale of priorities. Instead, they want more personal time so they can have a balanced life. A 33-year-old surveyed, who currently puts in 1,800 hours per year, said, "I don't want to work 2,200 hours a year, even if you paid me $100,000 more." Make time to relax. If you don't, the stresses that are part of life will overwhelm you and may even cause you to die a premature death. Bookstores and magazine racks abound with advice on this subject. It isn't my intention to try to compete with them in this chapter, but rather to give you a brief overview of what works for me and may work for you.

Let's start by explaining what people mean when they use the term "life balance." In a recent article in *Beyond Fitness* magazine, Laura Warf said, "Balance is more than a state of stability of the body. . . . It is also achieving a state of equilibrium at a mental, social, and spiritual level. It is important to our well-being to find balance between our physical, mental, spiritual, and emotional sides." And on www.5Pillars.com — The eCommunity for Balanced Living — they identify Body, Mind, Family, Society, and Finances as the keys to life balance, which is exactly in line with my own thinking. Both sources make it clear that each area is critical to achieving true balance in your life. When I reflect on some of the reasons for my numerous successes, I see that my lifestyle — rich in family, friends, fun, health, faith, and security — is the ideal recipe for a successful life. In the beginning, these may not have been conscious choices, but each has served to create the building blocks of a joyful life.

You can have all the money in the world, but if you are lacking in the other elements, you've failed to achieve true happiness. There are a lot of unhappy, unfulfilled millionaires and billionaires on the planet. Now, I don't mean to denigrate the value of financial security. People who live on the financial edge throughout their life are subject to incredible stress, which detracts from their ability to enjoy other aspects of their life. Similarly, I don't want to downplay the pleasure of having extra money to enjoy some of the fun things in life. My purpose in making these statements is to emphasize that acquiring money simply for its own sake is no guarantee you will have an enjoyable life. There's no doubt we live in a very stress-inducing world, and stress will deplete your happiness quotient. Whether it's stress related to events in your personal life or stress caused by the bombardment of bad news about crime, disasters, and horrors occurring around the globe, you still have to find ways to deal with it. Experts say there are three main ways to deal with stress:

1. **Change your situation**
2. **Change your attitude**
3. **Take care of yourself**

In the September, 2004, *Globe and Mail* article "Learning to Be Happy," Dr. Kenford Nedd counsels people to learn that every day is a new day, ripe with possibilities. The disappointments of previous days are now in the past and shouldn't be allowed to interject themselves on today. Wake up refreshed, energized, and ready to take on the world. Children do this instinctively without having to be told, but most adults allow themselves to be mired in discontent so they never experience the energy that comes from feeling happy and optimistic.

Dr. Nedd advocates taking notice of those five or ten little things that occur through the day that put a smile on your face. Some call this "living in the moment." But many people put off feeling happy. They say things like, "When such and such a thing happens, then I'll be happy." Does that mean that if these particular things don't happen, they are doomed to a life of unhappiness? Sometimes, we let ourselves get so busy and so frazzled that we fail to appreciate the small pleasures in life. Try an experiment: Sit down in a sunny spot with a good cup of coffee or tea, and just savour the moment. Doesn't it feel good? Were those few minutes of peace worth the time they took out of your day and away from your endless "to do list"? Of course they were, because when you tackled those items on your list, you did so in an energetic, positive frame of mind. Creating a few rituals in your day can pay huge dividends.

It's amazing how much better you feel when your day goes well. It's been said that life is 20% of what happens to you and 80% of how you react to it. Instead of flying into a rage or getting depressed when something goes wrong, take the time to put it into perspective. Maybe even try to find some humour in the situation. A little laughter is a good antidote for stress.

Taking time out for a little pampering is another way of enjoying life. A recent magazine article titled "Catering to the New Metrosexual Traveller" explained that hotels worldwide have realized there is a new target market out there for spa services. The term metrosexual was coined to describe men who are willing to spend time and money on appearance and lifestyle. I'm willing to admit that I was ahead of the trend on this one. For years I have endured teasing from my friends about my changing hair colour, my willingness to use skin care products, and my enjoyment of spa services. These things help me relax and reduce stress, and make me feel great about myself.

In the same vein, surrounding yourself with the right people is another of Dr. Nedd's tips. Try to keep negative people as far away from your sphere as possible. You want people who are sincere, genuine, fun loving, and with positive attitudes around you at all times.

They will help provide the spark needed to improve the quality of your day.

Physical Health

Maintaining my physical health is of paramount importance to me. For over 25 years, I have found comfort, strength, and revitalization in working out at least nine hours a week at the gym. I've made it a priority and rarely let anything deter me from spending at least three hours doing serious, heart pumping, sweat-inducing cardio exercise. As I've gotten older and am in a position to make a little extra time for myself, I often increase this schedule. The euphoria I feel after a good workout is hard to describe. I feel strong, energetic, and able to tackle any challenge. On the few odd occasions when my schedule has been disrupted, I suffer from exercise withdrawal. I feel out of sorts and out of shape with just a couple of missed sessions, so I do everything in my power to ensure that it doesn't occur too often. The other benefit of working out is it allows me to enjoy the pleasure of a good meal, even one with dessert and maybe a couple of glasses of wine, without worrying about gaining weight. I've been told by my doctor that my physical age is well below that of my chronological one, and people many years younger find they can hardly keep up with my hectic pace.

This brings to mind another point. Earlier in the chapter, I talked about savouring some daily moments of pleasure. Why not apply that to your exercise routine? Instead of watching the timer, wishing the minutes away, why not really focus on what you are doing and how much it is benefiting your health, and enjoy the effort you are making? I know that's what I consciously do nowadays. I recognize that the day may come when I will no longer be able to work out with the same vigour. When that happens I'm sure that I would give anything to be where I am today. So don't consider exercise a chore, look at it as something good you are doing for yourself.

Mental Health

Emotional health is also necessary for success and happiness. Lucy MacDonald called it "emotional fitness" in an article, saying: "Emotional fitness is an expression of how we feel about ourselves, others, and our ability to meet the demands of life. Positive emotional fitness helps us to maintain fulfilling relationships, to be productive, to adapt to change, and to cope with adversity." I've known a number of people who achieved a good measure of business success but who never reached their full potential because they were lacking in this area. They are the types of people who became abusive to others, thus destroying relationships, or were unable to cope when they couldn't have everything their own way. Irrational temper tantrums, retaliatory actions, depression, and sometimes the inability to make decisions are all symptoms of someone in poor emotional health. If you think this describes you, then I encourage you to get some professional help.

Community Involvement

I am a firm believer in the importance of giving something back to the community where you live and do terms of personal satisfaction when you make an effort to give something to your community.

Spiritual Health

Spirituality is a word that we hear more often today than we did over the past couple of decades. I think one reason is that people are beginning to appreciate the comfort that can be derived from a belief in something beyond our world. Sometimes you also hear people talk about faith. To many, faith is a foreign concept, but I think Madeleine L'Engle said it best: "Faith is what makes life bearable, with all its tragedies, and ambiguities, and sudden startling joys."

It doesn't necessarily mean you have to be religious to be a spiritual person. In my case, because of my deep-seated roots growing up as a Roman Catholic, it does translate into a belief in God. I was educated by a teaching order of priests, and then the time I spent at the seminary studying for the priesthood only served to cement my belief in God. I learned you should make a pact with yourself to act on faith and to let your decisions be guided by your deepest beliefs. You have to trust that the outcome will be for the greatest good. The power of prayer is something I learned from my earliest exposure to the Church, and I've had it reinforced over the years as my faith deepened. If praying is something you are not accustomed to, it will feel a little strange, but I can tell you that it's a very comforting ritual. There's something peaceful about sharing your innermost thoughts either vocally or mentally, knowing there is no judgement forthcoming. It gives you the opportunity to say or think what you might be afraid to business. While it is true that being a good corporate citizen can be beneficial to a company's reputation, this should not be the driving force behind your involvement. Years ago, I became one of the founding members of an organization called Best Buddies Canada. This group teams up mentally challenged adults with university students in order to form unique and mutually reward-ing friendships. I suspect my earlier, positive experience teaching young people probably drew me to this organization.

Giving of your time as a volunteer or board member is every bit as important as making financial donations. When local business leaders are actively involved in charitable activities, they become role models for other citizens in the community. All through my career I have encouraged our employees, managers, and partners to look for organizations and causes where they can make a worthwhile contribution. One person who really embraced this concept was Darryl Amirault in Halifax. Darryl and his group have been recognized numerous times for their outstanding community work. One charity, the MS Society of Canada, has presented them with a number of awards and has considered them to be a cornerstone in their fundraising efforts in Nova Scotia.

Similarily, my brother Terry is well known in Calgary as the person who is first in line to volunteer his assistance to any organization in need of help. On a more personal level, I also believe that once you are financially able to, it is important to donate money to help those members of your community who need a hand. There is no shortage of worthwhile causes and organizations all across this great country. You may be very surprised at how much you end up getting back in give voice to in a secular world. If the idea of praying is just too far out there for you, writing your thoughts down in a journal is another option. The idea is to create a venue where you can be totally honest with yourself. It's quite a liberating experience.

Taking time for meditation and reflection is not always easy, but I make an effort to do so. I have found this practice makes me more aware of what is good about my life, including the people in it. It makes me grateful for all my blessings and more desirous of helping others less fortunate. I've arrived at a stage in life when I can take a little time to be more introspective. I'd encourage everyone to do the same. We all know it isn't always a nice world out there, and if you don't make an effort to count your blessings, you can easily fall into the trap of cynicism. You should do your utmost to believe in the basic goodness of people and to give them the benefit of the doubt. Certainly, some will disappoint you but you can't let that make you suspicious of everyone. If you do, you will miss out on the joy of friendship and a sense of community with your fellow citizens.

A couple of weeks following the Asian Tsunami disaster on December 26, 2004, I attended mass and received a copy of that week's newsletter. In it was an open letter that really made me stop and think. The extent of this disaster is so overwhelming that humankind will be talking about it for decades to come. We in the developed world are so fortunate, yet we often take our blessings for granted. We even dare to complain when we think life isn't perfect. As successful businesspeople, we have a responsibility to think of others less fortunate. I'd like to share what I read in the newsletter.

It put things into proper perspective, and I think it will resonate with you as it did with me.

Food for Thought,
Apology to those in Developing Countries

While I was deciding which oat bran cereal to eat this morning, you were searching the ground for leftover grains from the passing wheat truck. While I was choosing between diet and regular soda, your parched lips were yearning for a sip of clean water. While I complained about the poor service in the gourmet restaurant, you were gratefully eating a bowl of rice. While I poured my "fresh and better" detergent into the washing machine, you stood in the river with your bundle of clothes. While I read the newspaper and drank my cup of steaming coffee, you walked the long, dusty miles to a crowded schoolroom to learn how to read. While I scanned the ads for a bargain on an extra piece of clothing, you woke up and put on the same shirt and pants that you have worn for many months. While I built a 14-room house for the three of us, your family of ten found shelter in a one-room hut. While I went to church last Sunday and felt more than slightly bored, you stood on the land with those around you and felt gratitude to God for being alive, one more day.

My brothers and sisters, forgive me for my arrogance and my indifference. Forgive me for my greed of always wanting newer, bigger, and better things. Forgive me for not doing my part to change the unjust systems that keep you suffering and impoverished.

— *Anonymous*

The topics discussed in this chapter are obviously very personal. I certainly can't do justice to them in these few pages, but I wanted to give you some non-business "food for thought." It is far too easy to get caught up in the daily grind or in the pursuit of making the next dollar. I know there have been occasions throughout my life when I have been as guilty of this as the next person. However, I've made an effort to truly understand that the things that are most important in life cannot be measured by material success, power, or recognition. To reach your full potential as a human being, it is essential to pay attention to family and health. If you do, happiness will follow.

KEY LESSONS LEARNED

- Strive to achieve a balance in your life — this includes physical and emotional health
- Avoid becoming a workaholic
- Make time for fun and adventure
- Live in the moment, enjoy the little things in life
- Giving to others is its own reward

CHAPTER FIFTEEN

FIFTY TIPS FOR THE SUCCESSFUL ENTREPRENEUR

"If you want to stand out, don't just be different, be outstanding."
— Meredith West

Being a successful entrepreneur means paying daily attention to so many different things. Whether it's dealing with clients, employees, or suppliers, the way each encounter is handled will have an impact on you and your business. This impact can be positive or negative — it's really up to you to decide which it will be. Throughout my career, I have discovered a wonderful secret in this regard. I have learned that more often than not, it's the little things that make the difference between success and failure. How you conduct yourself on a daily basis will determine how well you'll do in business and in life.

Whatever you do in life, do it right the first time and do it with the kind of style and class that will wow your friends, clients, and business associates. Don't settle for being mediocre or predictable. It may not be fair, but people judge others and companies by the impression they make. This extends to your personal appearance and that of your employees, the state of your business premises, and the manner in which you conduct yourself.

I would also like to take this opportunity to talk about change. Once you get your business up and running, you might be tempted not to make any changes in your operation — especially if things are going well. However, I'd like you to consider the premise that change is good and is, in fact, very desirable. Most people fear change, but I believe you must embrace change and learn to love it. In fact, I would go one step further and say *create change.* When constant change is part of your corporate culture, your employees will always be at the top of their game or they won't be able to survive in your organization.

My partners often tease me about my desire to change things, especially when everything is going well. The fact is, I believe the best time to change is when you are on the crest of the wave, not when you are in the trough. Most people believe that change should only happen when the company is in trouble. While it's true that in times of difficulty change may be necessary, change for the sake of shaking things up can be extremely positive. Without change, people can fall into a rut. The excitement fades and the energy departs. That's not what you want when you are trying to run a dynamic, leading edge company.

In his bestselling book, *If It Ain't Broke . . . Break It,* author Robert J. Kriegel said, "Leaders who stick with conventional formulas will not only miss great opportunities but will find their organizations struggling in the backwash." This is a place I never wanted our companies to find themselves in, which may explain why I am such an advocate of initiating change.

We live in a world of fast-paced change. Products or services that were once household names have disappeared from the marketplace. Many great companies died an undignified death because they refused to deal with reality. Customers today are a demanding group. They expect first-class service at very competitive prices. You have to be prepared to go that extra mile and do things differently if you are going to survive and thrive.

Many of the suggestions in this book have been encapsulated into the "50 Tips" presented below. These tips are not new and not particularly difficult, but they do work. Too often we are tempted to ignore the basics in favour of the "flavour of the month" business trend. Interestingly, many of these trends are simply old ideas dressed up in a new suit of clothes. I have tried my best to put these basic tenets into practice on a daily basis. Sometimes it would be easier to take some shortcuts or spend less time tending to employees, but I know that if I want to continue getting the kind of results I have achieved over the years, I must do the good things on a consistent basis. I encourage you to take at least a few of these suggestions to heart. You might be very surprised at how well they work and how quickly they will become second nature to you.

1. Make a great first impression. That means a strong handshake (for both men and women), a smile, and good eye contact to create an immediate connection. Always exude confidence.

2. Develop an effective phone manner. Be friendly, with good voice modulation. Start out with a more serious tone. If the caller is a friend or a close business associate, you can easily switch to a more jocular tone.

Personalize your greeting, such as using "Good afternoon" or "Good day." Learn to terminate calls quickly but politely, unless the caller is a customer. Give customers all the time they want. Speak clearly, and never mumble.

3. Be a high energy kind of person. At all times, move and talk quickly. It helps to convey confidence.

4. Never brag about your position, wealth, or possessions to employees, clients, or people in general.

5. Dress for success. Buy the absolute best you can afford. Remember, good clothes are an investment in your image.

6. Create a signature or unique look so that people will remember you (suspenders, crazy ties, cowboy boots, unusual jewellery, etc.).

7. Learn to remember names and faces. Use people's first names often in their presence. People love to hear their own name.

8. Always pay your own way. Be the first one to take out your credit card, unless you feel someone is taking advantage of you.

9. Always pay for everything when out with clients. They are your guests. Treat them well so they understand how much you appreciate their business.

10. Learn to deliver a sincere compliment and learn to accept a compliment in a gracious manner. If you act as if you didn't deserve such praise, people will come to agree with you.

11. Be on a first name basis with clients, staff, and service providers. Never consider yourself to be more important than another individual. Every person is worthy of respect.

12. Walk your office or facility floor each day. Speak to each

employee. Be accessible to employees. Have an open door policy. Listen to their opinions and ideas. Encourage creativity, diversity, and individuality.

13. Your time is your clients' time. You can never be too busy to accept their calls, even if you are in a meeting. Always stay in touch with former clients, even if they move on to another position or retire. Make sure they know that you value them as a person, not just as a source of business.

14. When it comes to a good work ethic, lead by example. You expect your employees to work hard. Show them that you are prepared to do the same. Never ask an employee to do a job you wouldn't do yourself. If possible, take some time away from the executive suite to work alongside your employees. It's good for morale.

15. Teach your employees to appreciate all of your customers, even those who are difficult. Develop a customer oriented culture. Employees who can't function in this manner should not be part of your team.

16. Have sales meetings twice a month. Set goals and share successes. Ask for input. Have staff meetings at least once a month, allowing different people to chair, in turn.

17. Share responsibility for making arrangements and setting agendas for major functions, including annual meetings or conventions. Share honours and kudos. Don't expect to be front and centre all the time.

18. Celebrate when your company receives an award or other form of public recognition. Make a point of congratulating and thanking all the employees. Make it an exciting event. Thank employees for their contribution to making it happen.

19. Only hire people with a great attitude, a genuine and sincere personality. Make sure they have a great work

ethic and a positive attitude. Avoid negative people at all costs. They will infect your workplace like a virus if they get a foothold.

20. Hire people whom other people want or hold in high regard. Make sure they know you appreciate having them on your team. Never make false promises at hiring time only to renege after they have joined your company.

21. Pay people what they are worth. Provide incentives for outstanding performance.

22. Hire lots of salespeople, but make sure they produce and pay their way. Don't keep non-producing salespeople around too long. Motivate and coach them, but if nothing changes, cut your losses.

23. Remember that every person who comes through your office door is a potential customer. Make sure they're greeted in a friendly manner and offered refreshments.

24. Don't depend on advertisements or employment agencies for new hires. Make it known to employees and clients that you are always on the lookout for great people. Provide incentives for referrals that work out.

25. Use tax-free gift certificates as bonuses (e.g., for clothing, travel, or spa treatments).

26. Get close to your employees. Learn something about their personal lives. This is particularly important with managers and partners. Don't be afraid to express your emotions in front of employees and they will respond in kind. Be affectionate with employees.

27. Keep your company's turnover rate as low as possible by creating a positive work environment and having a genuine interest in your employees' well-being.

28. Encourage professional development. Send staff on courses to improve their skills.

29. Return calls. There's nothing ruder than ignoring people.

If you are genuinely too busy to do this personally, then delegate someone to return the call on your behalf. Ensure that every caller knows you will personally follow up as soon as you are available.

30. Be punctual. Make a point of being at least five to ten minutes early for an appointment. Being one minute late for a client meeting is unacceptable. Always respect the other person's time. If you are unavoidably delayed, be sure to call ahead to advise and apologize.

31. Improve your manners. Take time to learn about proper etiquette. Be polite, mannerly, and humble at all times.

32. Be accessible to clients after normal business hours. Give them your home telephone number and your cell phone number. Take calls in the evenings or on weekends.

33. Sacrifice some of your privacy to bring people into your personal life. Invite them to your home. Introduce them to your family. Make them part of your circle.

34. Share confidential information with people you trust, especially clients and staff. Don't be secretive. It makes people feel good to know they are being trusted with "inside" information.

35. Always be honest and true to your word. Don't renege on promises. Conduct all business dealings with the utmost integrity.

36. Avoid lawsuits, even if you are in the right. No one wins in a lawsuit, and being involved in one takes your focus away from what you should be doing to manage your business.

37. Be prepared to personally provide exceptional service to clients. Make it a practice to personally follow up on any quotes or bids that your company has submitted for major contracts. Make sure the client involved understands that the president of the company is available to

them, not just the salesperson with whom they initially dealt.

38. Never avoid problems. Deal with them quickly and efficiently. Don't procrastinate. Make a decision and deal with issues immediately.

39. Make a "One Hour Rule" for dealing with customer complaints. Ensure that someone returns the customer's call within one hour to at least let them know you are working on resolving their problem. Assure them that a solution will be forthcoming in a timely manner.

40. If you need to follow up with someone, tell them to call you back by a specific date and time if they haven't heard back from you.

41. Don't be afraid to make decisions. If you have a good batting average, you'll be okay. If you make a wrong decision, be willing to live with the consequences. Remember, most business decisions are not brain surgery. No one will die if you make a wrong one.

42. Life isn't a personality contest. I believe that if 80% of people like and respect you, it's not necessary to worry about the other 20%.

43. Be a friend to the competition. Get to know them. Exchange ideas. Be willing to share information and opinions. You never know when you might want one of them as an employee or partner.

44. Treat all the people in your organization the same. Don't blatantly show favouritism. Be consistent in the application of rules or discipline.

45. Never show anger. We all get angry at times, but it is important to maintain a cool, calm, and collected demeanour. "Losing it" only hurts you.

46. Never burn bridges or harbour personal resentment.

47. As the leader of your company, it is your responsibility

to create a corporate culture that is based on respect and friendship.

48. Encourage your employees to enjoy each other's company. People who are friends are unlikely to want to leave. Retaining these people adds continuity to the company.

49. Have a connection to your community. It is imperative for you to give something back to the cities and towns where you do business. Choose an official corporate charity or charities. Volunteer to be on charity boards. Make charitable donations.

50. Have fun. Laugh every day. Love your people. Enjoy absolutely every minute of being an entrepreneur.

A NEW DAY DAWNS
THE BIRTH OF
PREMIERE VAN LINES

"When you go after something, go after it with everything you have. Push
yourself to the very edge."
— Greg Norman

I have devoted most of my adult life to the starting and
building of various business enterprises. Over the years
I have been privileged to have worked with a huge con-
tingent of wonderful people. These talented, hard-
working, caring, and affectionate human beings made
every moment worthwhile.

Entrepreneurs are among the most fortunate of all
businesspeople. We are the ones who can control our
own destiny. We can choose who we want to work with
and decide how that work will be done. I urge you to
choose wisely. I think I have managed to do so, not
because I am smarter than the next person, but because
I understood that no one person can do it all on their
own. You need to let others, many of whom will have
skills and talents that you are lacking, share in making
your business a success. When you have a core group of
people who believe in your company and in you as their

leader, there is no limit to what you can accomplish. I know this from personal experience.

My various business enterprises have also received a significant amount of public recognition and attention from the media. We have received awards, have had articles written about us, have appeared in radio and television interviews, and have been profiled in books. This kind of recognition helps a company to bolster its image within the business community and with the general public. It also makes the employees feel proud to be part of the organization. And it certainly gives the competition something to talk about. I will be honest and tell you that we actively sought out publicity. This is what a company must do to help market itself. I did it then and I will certainly continue to do it in the future. You would be wise to consider doing the same.

There is some irony in the fact that the new company I am part of, Premiere Van Lines, will be competing head-to-head with my former company. I know that we are not the first group of people to do something like this. It's happened in many other industries. If you had asked me a year ago if I would be starting a new national moving company at this point in my life, I would have said no. But when the friends who spent so many years helping me turn a dream into a reality asked for my help, I couldn't say no.

The idea for this new company began without my involvement. It was a well thought-out plan by the time I came into the picture. In fact, it started with a grass-roots movement headed up by franchisee Joe Boudreau of Sydney, Nova Scotia. Joe knew that many of his fellow franchisees were unhappy with the new management of my former company, and so he brought them together as a group. In order to ensure that their issues would receive a fair and respectful hearing, the group decided to retain the services of a renowned lawyer, the Hon. Larry Freeman of the prestigious law firm McInnis Cooper in Halifax, to act on their behalf during negotiations.

The group wanted the franchisor to know the time had come to pay serious attention to the issues and concerns raised by many of their franchisees. At that point, they had not yet decided to leave the organization. Unfortunately, the negotiations did not go well. The final outcome was the departure of 17 franchisees from the organization they had been associated with for many years. In my opinion, the group displayed an unbelievable degree of courage in sticking together. They managed to reject self-interest in favour of what was best for the group as a whole. This bodes well for their future as members of the Premiere Van Lines cooperative.

My ties to these people were stronger than my desire to stay out of the conflict. Thus, I made a life-changing decision to be part of the group's plans to start a new company, one in which they could re-create the culture they so dearly missed. My wife and I relocated to Toronto in January 2005. Doing so meant sacrificing our idyllic east coast lifestyle, but it was a sacrifice we were willing to make to repay the people who had always been there for us when we needed them.

While it is true that my involvement in Premiere Van Lines came from my desire to help my friends, I must also admit that as plans evolved I became very excited about this new opportunity. Former clients and other business associates have offered encouragement and support for our new venture, which has been very gratifying.

A few detractors have told me the moving industry has changed dramatically, and that I will find it very difficult to achieve the same degree of success as I've done in the past. Frankly, I'm happy to take this on as a personal challenge. I say this mainly because I don't think the fundamentals have really changed that much. The formula used in the past is as valid today as it was 20 years ago.

As far as I am concerned, companies operated by talented and dedicated people, determined to provide a superior product to their customers, will manage to be successful regardless of the industry. There has always been competition and there will always be competition. That fact won't change. How you approach your marketplace is what makes the real difference between winners and losers.

During the interim period leading up to the launch of the new company, Joe Boudreau and Darryl Amirault acted as co-presidents. These men guided everyone through a turbulent and emotional time. Each member of the group worked long and hard to make the necessary transition within their own location. Dealing with all of the practical matters prior to the April 1, 2005 launch date and still running a business on a day-to-day basis was no easy feat. Changing one's corporate affiliation is an immense task, involving everything from ordering new letterhead and business cards to painting trucks, changing building signs, informing clients, changing advertising, recording new on-hold messages, and a myriad of other details. It's a credit to each of Premiere's members that everything got done in time.

This is an exciting time for me and for every member of the Premiere Van Lines group. By the time this book is published, we will have launched our new venture with 30 offices coast to coast, with revenues of $45–$50 million. We have just signed a 15-year, multi-million dollar deal with Atlas Van Lines. I've set a personal goal that will see us grow to 40 offices by the end of year one, with revenues increasing to $60 million, and further growth by the end of year two with 45 offices and $80–$100 million in revenue. Remember what I told you about the importance of setting specific, time-defined goals? Obviously, I am taking my own advice!

As you can see, once the entrepreneurial spirit is ignited, it burns bright for a lifetime. I hope this book might inspire at least a few ambitious people to head off down the "Entrepreneur Road." I can assure you that if you do, life will never be boring.